# 1,001
# Ways to
# Celebrate
# Christmas

### & Create Lasting
### Traditions

# 1,001
# Ways to
# Celebrate
# *Christmas*

### & Create Lasting
### Traditions

CIDER MILL
PRESS

BOOK
PUBLISHERS
KENNEBUNKPORT, MAINE

Christmas is undoubtedly the most wonderful time of the year. People are nicer to one another, the nights are illuminated with dazzling displays of lights, and kids everywhere sleep with sugar plums dancing in their heads as they wait for Christmas morning. Christmas vacation is a time beloved by workers and students everywhere, but once you've exhausted all your hot cocoa recipes, worn out your ugly sweaters, and your family members all reach for their phones, it can be hard to come up with new Christmas activities on the spot.

If you've ever found yourself losing the Christmas spirit as you struggle to piece together an activity the whole family will enjoy, you're not alone. While everyone has their own list of Christmas activities, once the weather gets colder and family time gets hedged in by the latest toy, newest gadget, or loudest video game, it can feel like you've lost the meaning of the season. And with a veritable excess of time spent with extended family members, everyone gets more than a little stir-crazy around Christmas—even Santa Claus has to fly around the world to keep himself sane during the holidays.

While you may find yourself drinking in every free moment with your family, with a constant barrage of commercialism knocking at the door, it can seem nearly impossible to get everyone back in the Christmas spirit. If the idea of trying to plan out your holidays has you ready to throw in the stocking, think again! From unplugged holiday activities centered around giving back to your community to scavenger hunts, crafts, recipes, games, and more aimed at creating Christmas memories that will last a lifetime, this book is sure to get you back in the Christmas groove before you know it.

You can use this Christmas wish list of activities as a step-by-step guide, or you can use it as a jumping off point for your own holiday miracle. After all, there are over 1,000 to choose from, so you're sure to find something that works for your family. With choices geared toward holiday lovers young and old, there are plenty of Christmas activities here to create laughter, bring you closer together, and add a sprinkle of joy to help you all make it through the dreary months of winter. Just like celebrating Christmas, there's no real wrong way to use this book. So flip to a list, check it twice, and celebrate Christmas like never before.

Christmas isn't
a frame

# just a day, it's of mind.

—*Miracle on 34th Street* (1947)

## 1

Paint clothespins
red and green and use them
to hang Christmas cards
or other decorations.

## 2

Order mince pies online
or make your own using
your favorite recipe.

## 3

Track Santa's journey around
the world on Christmas Eve
using noradsanta.org.

## 4

Play capture the flag
as a family. This becomes
even more fun in the snow, as
you can use snowballs to tag
people and build forts
for each team.

## 5

Have a Christmas
photo shoot. Ask a friend or
hire a photographer to take
some pictures of you and your
family looking festive. For a
light-hearted approach, have
a few photos of everyone
wearing ugly Christmas
sweaters or matching
Christmas pajamas.

## 6

Give your local mail
carrier a thank you gift
for all of their hard work
around the holidays.

## 7

Try a new type of beer
or wine pairing with your
Christmas meal. You might
uncover a new favorite.

## 8

Attend *The Nutcracker* ballet performance.

## 9

Make dried fruit slices. Cut a variety of oranges, lemons, limes, and grapefruit into ¼- to ⅛-inch thick slices. Heat the oven to 125°F. Place wire racks on cookie sheets and arrange the fruit slices on the racks. Allow the fruit to dry in the oven for 5 to 6 hours, or until the fruit has dried out completely. Some slices may need to be removed sooner than others as different fruits will dry out at different rates.

## 10

Read *Letters from Father Christmas* by J.R.R. Tolkien.

## 11

It's fun to take pictures on Christmas morning, but nothing beats being able to look back on old memories in the form of home videos. Capture a little bit of all of your Christmas activities this winter and edit them into one video.

## 12

Write messages from Santa for your kids leading up to Christmas Eve. You can use lemon juice (revealed by heat), white crayons on white paper, or even write the messages backward to add to the fun.

## 13

Play Pictionary on Christmas Eve.

# 14
## Bake grasshopper cookies.

### Ingredients
#### For the Cookies
2 sticks of unsalted butter
¼ cup granulated sugar
Yolk of 1 large egg, at room temperature
½ teaspoon pure vanilla extract
½ teaspoon baking powder
½ teaspoon salt
½ cup unsweetened cocoa powder
2 cups all-purpose flour
½ cup semisweet chocolate chips, melted

#### For the Filling
½ cup heavy cream
1½ tablespoons light corn syrup
¾ lb. quality white chocolate, minced
2 tablespoons unsalted butter
1 teaspoon pure mint extract
¼ teaspoon red or green food coloring (optional)

### Directions
- To make the cookies, place the butter and sugar in a mixing bowl and beat at low speed with a handheld mixer to combine. Increase the speed to high and beat until light and fluffy. Beat in the egg yolk, vanilla, baking powder, and salt and then slowly add the cocoa powder and flour. Beat until a stiff dough forms.

- Place the dough on a sheet of waxed paper and roll it into a log that is 2½ inches in diameter. Cover in plastic wrap and refrigerate for 2 hours. The dough will keep in the refrigerator for up to 2 days.

- To prepare the filling, place the cream and corn syrup in a small saucepan and bring to a simmer. Stir in the white chocolate, butter, and mint extract, cover the pan, and remove from heat. Allow mixture to sit for 5 minutes. Stir well and, if using, stir in food coloring. Heat over very low heat if chocolate still has lumps. Press a sheet of waxed paper onto the surface and refrigerate.

- Preheat the oven to 350°F. Line two baking sheets with parchment paper and cut the chilled dough into ½-inch thick slices. Place the cookies on the baking sheets, place them in the oven, and bake until the edges start to brown, about 10 minutes. Remove from the oven, let cool on the baking sheets for 2 minutes, and then place on a wire rack to cool completely.

- When the cookies are cool, dip them in the melted chocolate until completely coated. Place the cookies back on the baking sheet and place it in the refrigerator until the chocolate has hardened, about 20 minutes.

- Beat the filling with a handheld mixer on medium speed until it is light and fluffy. Place a dollop on the flat side of 1 cookie and top with the flat side of another cookie. Repeat until all the cookies have been used.

## 15

Go to a thrift store and look for old Christmas records or CDs to play around the house.

## 16

Visit a holiday bazaar.

## 17

Make your own family board game and play it during the holidays. Let the kids come up with the rules to help teach them about fairness.

## 18

Make a Christmas collage out of old holiday cards. You can do this with cards you've received, or copies of your own Christmas cards.

## 19

Read the poem "Christmas Carol" by Sara Teasdale.

## 20

Host a sock swap. Everyone brings a new pair of socks that are filled with small gifts and then wrapped. Place all the packages in the middle of the room and let everyone choose a package to unwrap. Draw names to decide whose turn it is to pick.

## 21

Make Shrinky Dink ornaments to decorate your Christmas tree. You can find Shrinky Dinks at most craft stores, just make sure you do a test to see how much the pictures will shrink beforehand.

## 22

Make your own edible Christmas trees using your favorite candies. You can either arrange the candies in the shape of a tree or create your own 3-D masterpiece using toothpicks and soft candies like gumdrops.

## 23

If you live nearby, go see the Rockettes at Radio City Music Hall in New York City.

## 24

Make a life-sized gingerbread house out of cardboard boxes and decorate with construction paper candy. This can be fun for kids to play in or be a relaxing Christmas retreat for your cat or dog.

## 25

If you live somewhere warm, go for a family bike ride wearing Santa hats. You can even sing Christmas carols while you bike if you want.

## 26

Watch *A Christmas Story* (1983).

## 27

Know someone who just moved? Offer to help them unpack or set up their Christmas decorations.

## 28

Offer to volunteer at any holiday events like concerts or musicals that are happening at your child's school during the holidays.

# 29
# Make stained glass cookies.

### Ingredients
- 2 sticks of unsalted butter
- ¾ cup granulated sugar
- ½ cup packed light brown sugar
- 1 large egg, at room temperature
- ½ teaspoon pure rum extract
- ½ teaspoon salt
- 3¼ cups all-purpose flour, plus more for dusting
- ½ lb. preferred hard candy

## Directions

- Place the butter and sugars in a mixing bowl and beat at low speed with a handheld mixer until combined. Increase the speed to high and beat until the mixture is light and fluffy. Add the egg, rum extract, and salt and beat for 1 minute. Slowly add the flour to the mixture and beat until it is a stiff dough.

- Divide the dough in half and wrap each half in plastic wrap. Press the pieces of dough into a pancake and refrigerate for 1 hour. The dough will keep in the refrigerator for up to 2 days.

- Place the hard candy in a resealable freezer bag and pound with a small saucepan until crushed. Preheat the oven to 350°F and line two baking sheets with parchment paper.

- Place the dough on a flour-dusted work surface and roll each piece out to a thickness of ¼ inch. Cut into the desired shapes with flour-dusted cookie cutters. Use smaller cutters to create designs inside of the cookies, fill holes with crushed candy, and transfer cookies to the baking sheets. Bake cookies until the edges start to brown, about 10 minutes. Remove the cookies from the oven, let rest on baking sheets for 2 minutes, and then set on wire racks to cool completely.

### 30
Watch *A Charlie Brown Christmas* (1965).

### 31
Cut your children's sandwiches into festive shapes to celebrate the season.

### 32
Have a family talent show Christmas Eve. Be sure to invite your extended family to join in.

### 33
Spread the Christmas spirit by wearing a Santa hat in public. You can find plenty of unique patterns and styles, or even ones that celebrate your favorite sports teams.

### 34
Have a holiday-themed pun contest.

### 35
Make paper bag puppets of your favorite Christmas characters using markers, string, and anything else you want.

### 36
Make a paper angel chain. Cut a piece of printer paper into a 5 x 12-inch strip. Fold the paper accordion-style in equal sections. With the cut edge on the right, draw the silhouette of half an angel so that their arm reaches the cut edge of the paper. Cut out the silhouette and unfold.

**37**
Make Christmas crowns together and wear them on Christmas Day.

**38**
Read *I Believe in Santa Claus* by Diane G. Adamson.

**39**
Join in the Christmas pickle tradition. Make or purchase an ornament in the shape of a pickle. Hide the ornament somewhere on the tree on Christmas Eve after everyone has gone to bed. The first person to find the ornament on Christmas morning receives an extra gift or gets to open the first present under the tree.

**40**
Who says handprint animals are for Thanksgiving? Make handprint reindeer by turning your handprints upside-down and only painting half of your thumb. Be sure to add antlers.

**41**
Watch the cake makers at a big box store decorate the holiday cakes and cookies.

**42**
Have a Christmas spelling bee. Here are a few words to get you started: wassail, poinsettia, mistletoe, neighborhood, sleigh.

# 43
## Make gingerbread men.

### Ingredients

1½ sticks of unsalted butter, at room temperature
½ cup packed light brown sugar
⅔ cup molasses
1 large egg, at room temperature
1 teaspoon baking soda
1 teaspoon ground ginger
1 teaspoon apple pie spice
½ teaspoon salt
½ teaspoon pure vanilla extract
¼ teaspoon black pepper
3 cups all-purpose flour, plus more for dusting
Frostings of choice, for decoration (optional)
Candies of choice, for decoration (optional)

### Directions

· Place the butter and brown sugar in a mixing bowl and beat at low speed with a handheld mixer until combined. Increase the speed to high and beat until the mixture is light and fluffy. Add the molasses, egg, baking soda, ginger, apple pie spice, salt, vanilla, and pepper and beat for 1 minute.

· Slowly add the flour to the mixture and beat until it is a stiff dough.

· Divide the dough in half and wrap each half in plastic wrap. Flatten each piece into a pancake and refrigerate for 1 hour. The dough will keep in the refrigerator for up to 2 days.

- Preheat the oven to 350°F and line two baking sheets with parchment paper. Place the dough on a flour-dusted work surface and roll to a thickness of ¼ inch. Dip cookie cutters in flour and cut the dough into desired shapes. Transfer the cookies to the baking sheets and bake until firm, about 10 minutes.

- Remove the cookies from the oven, let rest for 2 minutes, and then set on wire racks to cool completely. Decorate with frosting and candies, if desired.

### 44

Make dinner for your neighbors or invite them over for a festive family dinner.

### 45

Running out of space to store your Christmas cards? Make a chain out of paper clips and attach them to magnets for an easy hanging display.

### 46

Read *4,000 Years of Christmas* by Earl W. Count and Alice Lawson Count.

### 47

Have a three-legged-race by tying together two people's legs with scarves or garlands.

### 48

Christmas is the perfect time for kids to think about which toys they don't use anymore and might be willing to donate. Keep your eyes open for toy drives in your area or donate to a thrift store.

### 49

Decorate a room in your home with paper snowflakes hanging from the ceiling for an indoor winter wonderland.

### 50

Avoid hearing the same annoying Christmas songs over and over on the radio by making a playlist of your favorites to listen to whenever you want.

### 51

Ask one family member to prepare a special toast to read before your Christmas dinner. It will become a fun tradition to see what people choose to give their toast about each year.

### 52

Make Christmas ornaments out of fuse beads.

### 53

Have an unlikely shopping date. Make a plan to go shopping with an in-law or relative you don't get to spend a lot of one-on-one time with. Not only will they be glad for the help in picking out gifts, it will also be a nice opportunity to spend quality time together.

### 54

Play holiday bingo. Create a list of 10 to 15 Christmas activities and give each guest the list. They have to then go around the room and find members who have done the activities on the list this year and check them off. Whoever fills in their list with a different person for each activity first, wins.

### 55

Take pictures of all of the things that inspire you this Christmas like decorations, food, and desserts, and look through them next year for ideas.

### 56

Watch *Klaus* (2019).

The best way
christmas cheer
for all

to spread
is singing loud
to hear.

—*Elf* (2008)

# 57
## Make this delicious sangria to serve at your next Christmas Party.

### Ingredients
- 1 (750 ml) bottle of dry red wine
- 1 orange, sliced into thin rounds, half-rounds, or wedges
- 2 Granny Smith apples, cored and seeded, cut into bite-sized pieces
- ¼ cup apple vodka
- ¼ cup brandy
- 1 (12 oz.) can lemon-lime soda

### Directions
- Combine all ingredients, except the soda, in a large pitcher or container. Cover and refrigerate for 4 or more hours. Add ice and soda. Stir and serve.

# 58
# Make your own beeswax food wraps to give as gifts.

## Tools
Sheets of washed cotton fabric, cut to
desired size
Cosmetic-grade beeswax pellets
Parchment paper
An iron

## Directions
- Begin by laying a piece of parchment paper
down on your ironing surface and placing
your fabric on top so that the reverse side
of the fabric is facing up. Cover the fabric with
an even layer of beeswax pellets, so that the entire surface
is covered. Make sure the pellets go all the way to the edge of the
fabric. Place another sheet of parchment paper on the top and iron over
it until the beeswax has melted.

- The beeswax will melt and can become runny. Make sure the parchment
is large enough to protect your ironing surface. Once the pellets have
melted, remove the top piece of parchment and carefully lift the fabric
away from the bottom piece of fabric. The fabric may need to cool for
one or two seconds before lifting.

- Hold the fabric in the air to allow the beeswax to dry. Wraps can be
cleaned by wiping the waxed side with a wet cloth.

**59**

Christmas is the perfect time to try your hand at making and selling crafts or baked goods. Sign up for a booth at your local craft fair this year.

**60**

Stay in a cabin over the holidays.

**61**

Create your own wrapping paper patterns using apples. Cut the apples in half and dip in paint as-is or carve them into unique shapes before applying the paint.

**62**

Take your kids to Christmas story time at your local library.

**63**

Make a stop motion holiday film together.

**64**

Give everyone in your family wool socks to help them stay warm.

**65**

Use Christmas as an excuse to replace all of the silverware in your home with a new, matching set.

**66**

Read "The Adventure of the Blue Carbuncle" by Arthur Conan Doyle.

**67**

Make s'mores around a campfire.

### 68

Who says dressing up is just for Halloween? Bring your Christmas party to life by having a dress up contest. Have everyone come dressed as a Christmas themed character and give a prize to the most creative costume.

### 69

Make handprint Santas by covering your fingers in white paint, the center of your palm in whatever skin tone paint you prefer, add a streak of white for the edge of the hat near the bottom of your palm, and cover the base of your hand and thumb in red paint for the hat. Press onto a piece of paper, add in eyes, outline the hat, and display.

### 70

Start the holiday season and the new year on the right foot by going through your closets and donating anything that you no longer use to charity.

### 71

For interesting insight into different Christmas traditions, listen to the podcast *Christmas Past*.

### 72

Enter a gingerbread house contest. This can be a fun way to push your gingerbread house to the next level and make something really creative. Can't find any contests near you? Start your own.

# 73
## Make peppermint bark.

### Ingredients
- ¾ cup crushed peppermint candies
- ¾ lb. semisweet chocolate chips
- 2 teaspoons vegetable oil
- ¾ lb. white chocolate chips

## Directions

- Line a rimmed baking sheet with parchment paper and place the crushed peppermint candies in a mixing bowl.

- Place the semisweet chocolate chips in a microwave-safe bowl. Microwave on medium until melted, removing to stir every 20 seconds.

- Stir 1 teaspoon of the vegetable oil into the melted chocolate and then pour the chocolate onto the baking sheet, using a rubber spatula to distribute evenly. Place in the refrigerator until set, about 15 minutes.

- Place the white chocolate chips in a microwave-safe bowl. Microwave on medium until melted, removing to stir every 20 seconds. Add the remaining oil, stir to combine, and pour the melted white chocolate on top of the hardened semisweet chocolate, using a rubber spatula to distribute evenly.

- Sprinkle the peppermint pieces liberally over the white chocolate and lightly press into the chocolate. Refrigerate until set, about 30 minutes. Break the bark into pieces and refrigerate until ready to serve.

**Tip:** Arrange in a tin or stack pieces in a clear plastic bag and tie with ribbon for a memorable Christmas gift.

## 74

If you live somewhere cold, make your own snow with boiling water. This should only be done by adults. When the temperature outside is at -22°F (-30°C), throw boiling water into the air. The water will turn into snow in midair!

## 75

Play musical chairs using your favorite Christmas music.

## 76

Fill your house with nature. The season for fresh cut flowers might be long gone, but that doesn't mean you can't fill vases with sprigs of pine, holly, and bittersweet.

## 77

Go "phone caroling" by calling friends and family and leaving Christmas carol voicemails.

## 78

Have a contest to see who can come up with the most unique Christmas gift.

## 79

Make a hot toddy. In a mug, combine 1 oz. bourbon, 1 tablespoon honey, and 2 teaspoons lemon juice, then pour ½ cup boiling water into the mug, and stir to combine. Garnish with a slice of lemon and a cinnamon stick.

## 80

Attend an ice sculpture contest. You don't have to participate; it can be just as fun watching the sculptures come to life.

## 81

Take the stress out of the holidays by turning your living room into a spa complete with cucumber slices and relaxing music.

## 82

Make tissue paper snowflakes. If you hang these snowflakes in the windows, the sun will shine through the paper for an eye-catching effect.

## 83

Make a homemade terrarium and give it as a gift. Choose a container that is right for your plants and fill the bottom with a layer of gravel for good drainage. Make sure you keep in mind planting instructions for the specific plants when designing your terrarium. You can make your terrarium Christmas-themed by adding small Christmas decorations.

## 84

Decorate a wreath with foraged materials from your backyard or local park. Find sprigs of bittersweet, feathers, cattails, acorns, or other natural curiosities to make a wreath that really stands out.

# 85

## Make a peppermint party cake using leftover peppermint bark.

### Ingredients
#### For the Cake

- 3¼ cups flour, plus more for dusting
- 2½ teaspoons baking powder
- 1 teaspoon salt
- ¾ cup unsalted butter, at room temperature
- 2 cups granulated sugar
- 1¼ cups milk, warmed to room temperature
- 2 teaspoons vanilla extract
- 4 large eggs

#### For the Frosting
- 1 stick of unsalted butter, softened and cut into fourths
- 2 cups confectioners' sugar
- 1½ teaspoons vanilla extract
- 2 tablespoons whole milk, at room temperature

#### For the Topping
- ½ to ¾ cup peppermint bark (see page 30), broken into walnut-sized pieces or smaller
- 5 to 6 peppermint candies

## Directions

- Preheat oven to 350°F. Lightly grease and flour two 9 x 2-inch round cake pans.

- To prepare the cake, in a bowl, whisk together the flour, baking powder, and salt. In a large bowl, beat the butter and sugar together on low speed until combined and crumbly. Add about ½ cup of the flour mixture, beating to combine, then add some of the warmed milk, alternating between the dry ingredients and the milk until combined and smooth, scraping the sides and bottom of the bowl. Add the vanilla.

- Blend in 1 egg at a time with the beaters on low, mixing until thoroughly combined. When all have been added, turn the mixer to medium and beat for another 30 seconds or so at the higher speed. Divide the batter between the two pans, tapping the bottoms to be sure the batter settles.

- Bake for 25 to 30 minutes until the cake is golden around the edges and a toothpick inserted in the middle comes out clean. Remove from the oven and put the pans on a wire rack to cool. Allow to cool thoroughly.

- To make the frosting, add the butter to a large bowl. Add about ½ cup of confectioners' sugar and, working with a large spoon, cream the butter and sugar together until smooth. Continue to stir in the sugar ½ cup at a time until fully combined. Add the vanilla and milk and continue to stir for about 2 to 3 minutes. The frosting should be soft and creamy.

- To make the topping, break the peppermint bark into pieces and set aside. Put the mints into a strong plastic bag and use a hammer or rolling pin to break them into shards.

- To assemble the cake, place one of the cooled cake layers on a plate. Spread about ½ cup frosting on top. Sprinkle with peppermint bark pieces, distributing evenly. Place the other layer of cake on top. Frost the sides, working from bottom to top. Frost the top last, then top the cake with the peppermint candy shards.

## 86

Make a Peppermint Mocha White Russian. Fill 2 cocktail glasses half full with crushed ice. Pour 1½ oz. of vodka and coffee liqueur into each. Add 1 oz. of half-and-half and vanilla almond milk to each one. Stir and garnish with pieces of peppermint bark.

## 87

Fill jars with your favorite holiday candy and give them as gifts.

## 88

If you live near the coast, find out if any lighthouses in your area are decorated for Christmas and take a drive to see one.

## 89

Grow an amaryllis. This particular bloom comes in red and white varieties, making it perfect for the holidays. Plant an amaryllis bulb of your choice in a heavy 6- to 8-inch pot. Fill the pot with potting soil and plant the bulb, pointed end up, so that ⅓ of the bulb sticks above the soil. Place the potted plant indoors in bright, indirect light. Water lightly at first until you can see about 2 inches of new growth, then water every time the soil in the pot feels dry. Be sure to rotate the pot as the stalk grows. For a Christmas bloom, you will want to plant your amaryllis around the last week of October.

### 90

Everyone knows that
pets are part of the family,
so why not give them the love
they deserve with their own
stocking this year? Make sure
Santa fills them with plenty of
healthy treats and fun toys.

### 91

Play pin the heart
on the Grinch.

### 92

If there is no free
meal program in your area,
try setting up your own free
community meal around the
holidays. You can ask for food
donations from stores and find
a local place to cook the
meal like a church or
community center.

### 93

See a play.

### 94

Be a holiday tourist in
your own town and try out
all the fun winter activities
your town has to offer.

### 95

Plant some holly bushes in
your yard. These bushes can
add to your landscaping year-
round but are especially festive
close to Christmas because
they remain green.

### 96

Buy cheap canvas
shoes and decorate them for
Christmas using fabric
paints or tie-dye.

# 97
# Make Christmas-themed slime.

## Ingredients
1 (5 to 6 oz.) bottle of clear glue
¾ teaspoon borax
1 cup hot water
½ cup room temperature or cold water
Red or green food coloring
Red or green glitter

## Directions
- In a large bowl, mix hot water with the borax until the borax has dissolved completely.

- In a separate bowl, mix the glue with the ½ cup of water. Stir until the water and glue have been completely incorporated. Add a few drops of food coloring and the desired amount of glitter to the glue mixture and stir to combine.

- Pour the glue into the borax mixture. With gloved hands, work the glue into the borax so it absorbs as much water and borax as possible. This will take a few minutes.

- Once the slime no longer feels sticky, remove from bowl. Transfer to an airtight container and store for up to one week.

# 98
# Make apple and spice sangria.

## Ingredients
1 Granny Smith apple, cored, seeded, peeled, and cut into bite-sized pieces
1 Empire apple, cored, seeded, peeled, and cut into bite-sized pieces
½ cup fresh cranberries
¼ cup cranberry juice
¼ cup apple cider
¼ cup apple vodka
Dash of nutmeg
1 (750 ml) bottle of sparkling wine, very cold

## Directions
- In a bowl, combine the apple pieces and cranberries. Pour the cranberry juice, apple cider, and apple vodka over the fruits. Add the dash of nutmeg and stir to combine. Cover and refrigerate for at least 2, and up to 6, hours.

- Remove from refrigerator and strain the juice into a measuring cup. Ladle two spoonfuls of fruit into 4 to 6 glasses. Pour equal amounts of the juice-and-vodka combination into each glass and top with sparkling wine, refilling as necessary.

Freshly cut
smelling of stars
pine resin—inhale
your soul with

# Christmas trees and snow and deeply and fill wintry night.

—John Geddes, *A Familiar Rain*

**99**

Make ice cubes in Christmas novelty ice cube trays.

**100**

Paint the outside of plain glass candle votives with nail polish and give them as gifts.

**101**

Use white crayons and paint to make cool contrast drawings of snow. This is especially fun if you use black paper.

**102**

Paint Christmas suncatchers. Check your local craft store for Christmas-themed suncatchers, and spend the afternoon painting them to hang in a winter window.

**103**

Go miniature golfing, weather permitting.

**104**

Play Christmas Scattergories. You can find plenty of lists online, or make up your own.

**105**

Watch *The Nativity Story* (2006).

**106**

Worried about your pets getting to your poinsettias? Make your own using red felt and pipe cleaners.

**107**

Wear jingle bell jewelry or accessories to celebrate the holidays.

## 108
Listen to *A Pentatonix Christmas*.

## 109
Watch *The Polar Express* (2004).

## 110
Make a festive tic-tac-toe board by stapling garlands to cardboard to make the board. You can decorate the edges of the board as well. Put a single thumb tack in the center of each square. Then, have two sets of ornaments, one for the "X"s and one for the "O"s. Each player takes their turn by hanging their ornament in the square they choose. This is a great game to keep going through the holidays.

## 111
Buy wrapping paper that is made from recycled materials.

## 112
Watch a Christmas parade. Check to see if your town or one nearby will be holding a parade this year.

## 113
Read *Pippi's After-Christmas Party* by Astrid Lindgren.

## 114
Make root beer floats. Place two scoops of vanilla ice cream at the bottom of each glass. Slowly pour root beer over the ice cream to prevent foaming, then top with whipped cream and serve.

# 115

## Make peppermint crunch truffles.

### Ingredients
- 1 cup peppermint candy, crushed into shards
- 14 oz. semisweet chocolate chips
- ¾ cup heavy cream
- ½ teaspoon vanilla extract
- ½ teaspoon peppermint extract
- 2 tablespoons unsalted butter, at room temperature
- Cocoa powder, for dusting

## Directions

- Put the peppermint candies in a strong plastic bag and use a hammer or rolling pin to crush them into shards. Set aside.

- In a double boiler or in a bowl over simmering water, heat chocolate chips until melted, stirring frequently.

- While the chocolate is melting, heat the cream in a saucepan over medium heat until it just starts to boil, stirring frequently. As soon as bubbles faintly emerge around the edges, remove from heat and whisk in the vanilla and peppermint extracts.

- Remove the melted chocolate from the double boiler. While the chocolate and cream are warm, slowly add the cream into the chocolate, stirring gently and incorporating it slowly. Once combined, add the butter and stir it in until melted. Cool to room temperature, and then cover with plastic wrap and refrigerate until hardened, about 4 to 5 hours.

- To make the truffles, line a large baking sheet with parchment paper. Take the chocolate out of the refrigerator and scoop using a teaspoon. Roll the chocolate in your hands, forming small balls. Dust your hands lightly with cocoa powder if they get too sticky.

- Once the balls are formed, put the peppermint candy shards in a pie plate. Roll each ball in the candy and then put it back on the wax paper-lined baking sheet.

### 116

Make a Cranberry Spice cocktail. Combine ¼ oz. Chambord, ½ oz. Domaine de Canton , ¼ oz. Cabernet Sauvignon, and 1 oz. cranberry juice in a cocktail shaker filled with ice and shake until chilled. Strain into a shot glass and garnish with 2 fresh cranberries, if desired.

### 117

Paint lines from your favorite holiday songs on Christmas ornaments.

### 118

Spruce up the gifts under your tree by adding some natural flair, like pinecones or sprigs of evergreen.

### 119

Make Christmas-themed Popsicles by freezing red and green juices in Popsicle molds. If you want to make multicolored Popsicles, pour one color juice in half the mold, allow to freeze, then add the other juice and freeze again.

### 120

Look into trains that run near you and see if you can work a trip into your holiday itinerary.

### 121

Have a '70s- or '80s-themed Christmas party. Take your Christmas party to the next level by having everyone break out their bell bottoms and leg warmers.

## 122
Read *The Christmas Alphabet* by Robert Sabuda.

## 123
Start a holiday-inspired collection. You can collect Santa figurines, nutcrackers, or even miniature Christmas trees.

## 124
Put electric candles in each window of your home and turn them on in the evenings so your house looks warm and festive from the street.

## 125
Have everyone wear Rudolph noses made from pom-poms for a Christmas photo.

## 126
Watch a movie that you forgot was a Christmas movie. Try one of these:
*Gremlins* (1984)
*Die Hard* (1988)
*Edward Scissorhands* (1990)
*Batman Returns* (1992)
*L.A. Confidential* (1997)
*Annie* (1999)
*Harry Potter and the Sorcerer's Stone* (2001)

## 127
Go ice skating at Rockefeller Center.

## 128
Make a Christmas bucket list of all the things you want to do before Christmas vacation ends.

# 129
# Make Christmas-scented perfume balm.

## Ingredients
- 2 to 3 sprigs of pine or juniper needles
- 6 tablespoons grapeseed oil
- 2 cinnamon sticks
- ½ teaspoon vanilla extract
- ¼ teaspoon nutmeg
- ½ teaspoon vitamin E oil
- ¾ cup cosmetic grade beeswax pellets

## Directions
- Gently bruise the pine or juniper needles with a wooden spoon. Pour oil into the bottom of a sealable glass container and add needles, cinnamon sticks, vanilla, and nutmeg.

- Use the spoon to gently stir ingredients so the oil coats everything. Seal the container and place in a cool spot, out of direct light. Using a tinted glass container can help protect ingredients from the light. Let rest for 1 to 2 weeks.

- Remove the lid and determine if the mixture has reached a desired potency. If the smell is too weak, strain the oil, discard needles and cinnamon, and add fresh, solid ingredients as desired. Reseal and leave for another week.

- Once the scent of the mixture has reached your desired strength, strain out the solids, stir in the vitamin E oil, and set aside.

- Melt beeswax pellets in a double boiler. When the beeswax has melted, add the scented oil and stir. While the wax is still hot, pour into a sealable metal or glass pot, and allow to harden with the lid off.

### 130

Decorate your backyard by placing red and green glow sticks in mason jars and leaving them outside in the snow. This is a great way to decorate without having to string up a bunch of lights.

### 131

Have a nineteenth-century Christmas. Decorate for Christmas and give gifts using only materials and resources that would have been available in the 1800s. This can be a good way to downsize your Christmas, and you will have fun coming up with old fashioned ways to celebrate (see popcorn garlands on page 110 and pomanders on page 79).

### 132

Make family silhouettes. Using a projector or bright flashlight, have someone sit in front of a blank piece of paper. Trace their silhouette, then remove and fill in however you want. You can make these more festive by all wearing antlers or a Santa hat, or by drawing ugly Christmas sweaters on everyone.

### 133

For a gift that keeps on giving, get your loved one a gym membership.

### 134

Paint plant pots with festive colors to give your houseplants a holiday makeover.

## 135

Working right up to the holidays is no fun, but you can keep the Christmas spirit alive by bringing decorations into your workspace. You can hang up lights, display Christmas cards, or even put a mini Christmas tree on your desk.

## 136

Make red and green tie-dye shirts.

## 137

Read the poem "Christmas Bells" by Henry Wadsworth Longfellow.

## 138

Visit New York City and see the Rockefeller Christmas Tree.

## 139

Spend the afternoon drinking hot chocolate and reading at a local café.

## 140

There are endless holiday festivals, craft fairs, concerts, parades, and other attractions that only pop up during the holidays. Make sure to search online to find out what's going on in your area.

## 141

Treat yourself to the ultimate night out by going to one restaurant for appetizers, then a new one for your main course, and then go somewhere else for dessert. This can work with fast food runs as well.

# 142
# Make chocolate and cinnamon brioche.

### Ingredients
¼ teaspoon active dry yeast
¼ teaspoon granulated sugar
1½ cups lukewarm water (90°F to 100°F)
2 sticks of unsalted butter, cut into small pieces
1 cup semisweet chocolate chips
1 teaspoon ground cinnamon
Yolks of 6 large eggs
1 teaspoon salt
3 cups all-purpose flour, plus more for dusting

### Directions
- Put the yeast and sugar in a measuring cup and add about ½ cup of the water in a drizzle. Cover the measuring cup with plastic wrap and set it aside for about 15 minutes. If the yeast doesn't foam, it is not alive and you'll need to start over.

- Place the butter and the chocolate chips in a microwave-safe bowl. Melt the chocolate and butter in the microwave on medium, removing to stir every 20 seconds. Remove, stir in the cinnamon, and let cool to room temperature.

- When the yeast is proofed, pour it into a large bowl and add the egg yolks and remaining water. Stir gently to combine. Combine the salt and the flour in a separate bowl, and then add to the yeast mixture. Stir with a wooden spoon until combined. The dough should be wet and sticky.

- Put a dusting of flour on a flat surface and lift out the dough. With flour on your hands and more at the ready, begin kneading the dough so that it loses its stickiness. Don't overdo it, and don't use too much flour—just enough that the dough becomes more cohesive. While kneading, add the chocolate-and-cinnamon mixture in small increments. Place the dough in a large bowl, cover the bowl with plastic wrap, and allow to rise for at least 1 hour. Gently punch it down, cover with the plastic, and allow to rise for another 30 minutes or so.

- While the dough is on its final rise, preheat the oven to 450°F. Put a piece of parchment paper on the bottom of a Dutch oven, cover it, and place it in the oven. When the oven is ready, use potholders to remove the lid of the Dutch oven, scoop the dough from the bowl to the pot, and bake with the lid on for 15 minutes. Remove the lid and bake for another 15 to 20 minutes, until the top is golden and the bread sounds hollow when tapped. Remove the pot from the oven and carefully remove the bread. Allow to cool before slicing.

### 143

Make a snowman kit. This makes a fun gift, or a nice treasure to keep at home for your own family. Find an old hat, pieces of polished coal or rocks for the eyes and mouth, sticks for the arms, and mittens for the hands, and store in a decorated bag. Just add snow and a carrot for the perfect snowman.

### 144

Make a tinfoil mosaic using wrapping paper, glue, and a piece of card stock. Have your kids draw the outline they want to fill in, then use the tinfoil and wrapping paper to color in different areas by rolling them into small pieces and gluing them to the paper.

### 145

Go birdwatching for winter birds.

### 146

Make a snowman windchime using old cans, white paint, pieces of felt for the eyes, nose, and buttons, and a ribbon for the scarf. To make the windchime, drill a hole in the bottom of each can and thread fishing line through the center. About halfway down each can, tie washers and nuts to the string to make the noise. Then, hang your snowman outside and enjoy.

### 147

Make holiday cards for hospital patients.

## 148

Get a seasonal job. Many businesses hire special temporary employees to help them through the rush of the holidays. This could be the perfect time to try out a new job, or simply make some extra money this Christmas.

## 149

Go 24 hours without the internet, TV, or your phone, and really enjoy your vacation.

## 150

Have a handmade-only Christmas. Agree as a family to only give gifts that you make by hand or buy handmade. This will force you to get creative and think of something really meaningful.

## 151

Read *Elf on the Shelf* and adopt your own Scout Elf.

## 152

If you have a tattoo-enthusiast in your life, chip in toward their next tattoo for a unique, long-lasting Christmas present.

## 153

Compost your Christmas tree when you are done enjoying it. Putting your tree through a woodchipper and then composting it is a healthy way to dispose of your tree and will benefit your garden.

Nothing ever hard, or too sad a Christmas tree

# seems too bad, too when you've got in the living room.

—J. D. Robb, *Memory in Death*

# 154
## Wow your holiday guests with gingerbread ice cream.

### Ingredients
1½ cups heavy cream
1½ cups whole milk
2 teaspoons ground ginger
2 teaspoons cinnamon
1 teaspoon nutmeg
¼ teaspoon ground cloves
2 tablespoons molasses
Pinch of salt
⅔ cup granulated sugar
Yolks of 5 eggs

### Directions
- Place all of the ingredients, except for the sugar and egg yolks, in a medium saucepan and cook over medium heat until the mixture starts to bubble. Remove from heat and let the mixture steep for 30 minutes to 1 hour.

- Strain, discard the solids, wipe out the saucepan, and return the liquid to it. Bring to a simmer over medium heat.

- Place the sugar and egg yolks in a bowl and whisk until combined. Add a little bit of the mixture in the saucepan to the eggs, while stirring constantly to keep from cooking the eggs.

- Add the tempered eggs to the saucepan and cook until the mixture is thick enough to coat the back of a wooden spoon. Remove from heat and let cool. Cover the pan and transfer to the refrigerator. Chill overnight.

- When you are ready to make the ice cream, place the mixture in your ice cream maker and churn until the desired texture is achieved. Freeze for at least 6 hours before serving.

## 155

Look up and make vintage candy recipes as a family.

## 156

Send some local flavor to a friend who has moved out of town. This could be your favorite local BBQ sauce, honey from a local farm, or a box of goodies from your favorite bakery.

## 157

Host a cooking contest at your family Christmas gathering. Set a theme like salsa, cookies, bread, or party mix, and have everyone who wants to participate bring their own version of the chosen dish. Then, have everyone at the party vote on which dish they like the best.

## 158

Make origami crane Christmas ornaments.

## 159

Play flashlight tag. This is also fun in the snow, just make sure to bundle up before heading outside.

## 160

Keep track of who in your family can spot the most wild animals outside in the snow during the month of December.

## 161

If you are planning a vacation for after Christmas, give your kids toys or books that will keep them entertained during travel.

## 162
Visit an ice bar near you.

## 163
Place Christmas-themed pinwheels in your front garden. Make pinwheels using squares of paper, brass fasteners, and straws. Simply take the squares of paper and fold in half to make a triangle shape, then unfold and fold the other direction to make another triangle. Cut halfway along the folds on each edge, then punch a hole in one corner of each of the cut triangles. Fasten the four corners in the center with a brass fastener, push through the middle of the paper, and press the fastener through the straw. Open the fastener to finish the pinwheel.

## 164
Live somewhere without snow? Cover your backyard slide with shaving cream and go "sledding" using pieces of cardboard. Be sure to wear your bathing suit for easy clean up, of course.

## 165
Make a hot chocolate bar. Fill a spot on the counter or a table with bowls of your favorite hot chocolate toppings and let everyone add what they'd like to their mugs.

## 166
Switch out your normal pens for festive gel pens during the holidays to add a touch of festivity to everything you write.

# 167
## Bake a classic apple pie.

Ingredients
8 cups peeled, cored, and sliced apples
2 tablespoons fresh lemon juice
½ cup granulated sugar
2 teaspoons cinnamon
Pinch of salt
¼ cup all-purpose flour, plus more for dusting
2 balls premade pie dough
1 egg, beaten

## Directions

- Place the apple slices, lemon juice, and sugar in a large saucepan and cook over medium heat until the apples are just beginning to soften.

- Add the cinnamon and salt and cook for another minute. Strain the mixture through a fine sieve, reserve the liquid, and place the apples in a mixing bowl.

- Return the reserved liquid to the saucepan, add the flour, and whisk to prevent lumps from forming. Cook until the liquid starts to thicken. Pour into the bowl containing the apples, stir to combine, and let cool completely. Preheat the oven to 450°F and grease a 9-inch pie plate.

- When the apple mixture is cool, place the balls of dough on a flour-dusted work surface and roll them out so that they fit the pie plate. Place one of the crusts in the prepared pie plate and then evenly distribute the apple mixture inside of the crust. Place the remaining crust on top, crimp to seal, and cut 4 to 5 slits in the center. Brush the beaten egg over the top crust.

- Place the pie in the oven and bake for 15 minutes. Reduce the temperature to 350°F and bake until the crust is golden brown and the filling is bubbling, about 30 minutes. Remove from the oven and let cool before serving.

## 168

Make your own holiday pop-up book by taking a small notebook and drawing a picture on a separate piece of paper. Cut this picture out and fold it down the middle. Take two different pieces of paper and glue them to each page individually, making sure they meet the edges of the drawing but not all the way to the center. Glue the pieces of paper to the picture, close the book, and then open it to see your new pop-up book.

## 169

Host a fancy dinner party in the weeks leading up to Christmas.

## 170

Paint a snowy scene on your window. You can purchase washable window paints or add a little dish soap to tempera paint. Make sure you use soap, not detergent, as detergent can damage the glass.

## 171

Have a festive fashion show with all your favorite Christmas-themed outfits. This includes ugly sweaters, PJs, and anything else you want to show off.

## 172

Many petting zoos host reindeer events during the winter months. Why not visit Santa's reindeer as a family?

### 173
Watch *Love, Actually* (2003).

### 174
Enjoy time with family this holiday season by escaping to the mountains for a weekend of skiing. Book early for the best rates on hotels and ski passes.

### 175
Go see a holiday musical.

### 176
Make glow-in-the-dark snow monsters by building snowmen and putting red and green glow sticks in their eyes or around their arms for a festive nighttime surprise.

### 177
Make thumbprint snowmen using white paint, markers, and any other craft supplies you want.

### 178
Make baked apples in a campfire. Use an apple corer to remove the center of each apple. Place individual apples on sheets of tin foil and fill the center with fillings of your choice. Wrap foil around the apple so it is completely covered. Place the wrapped apples on the embers of a campfire and cook for 5 to 10 minutes. Remove from fire and unwrap to let cool slightly. Enjoy with ice cream or whipped cream.

# 179
## Make Irish lamb stew for Christmas Eve dinner.

Ingredients
- 2 lbs. boneless lamb shoulder, cut into bite-sized cubes
- 2 bay leaves
- 6 Yukon gold potatoes, sliced ¼-inch thick
- 3 yellow onions, sliced
- 2 large rutabagas, peeled and sliced ¼-inch thick
- Salt and pepper, to taste
- 4 sprigs of parsley
- 2 large carrots, peeled and sliced ½-inch thick

### Directions

- Place the lamb and bay leaves in a large cast-iron Dutch oven and cover with cold water. Bring to a boil over high heat and cook for 5 minutes. Remove the lamb with a slotted spoon and set aside. Transfer the broth and bay leaves to a separate container.

- Place half of the potatoes in a layer at the bottom of the Dutch oven. Top with a layer of half of the onions and another layer consisting of half of the rutabagas. Add the lamb, season with salt and pepper, and top with the remaining potatoes, onions, and rutabagas. Add the broth and bay leaves and bring to a boil. Reduce heat so the stew simmers, cover, and cook for 1 hour.

- Remove the lid, add the parsley and carrots, and simmer for another hour. Remove the parsley and bay leaves and ladle the stew into warmed bowls.

### 180
Listen to a Christmas album by Trans-Siberian Orchestra.

### 181
If you live somewhere without ice skating, visit a roller-skating rink instead.

### 182
Instead of a big dinner, why not put together a spread of your favorite breakfast and lunch treats for a Christmas brunch?

### 183
Drink hot chocolate around an outdoor campfire.

### 184
Read *The Velveteen Rabbit* by Margery Williams Bianco.

### 185
Read the poem "[little tree]" by E. E. cummings.

### 186
Watch *The Santa Clause 3* (2006).

### 187
Bring a hand-decorated wreath into work to share some holiday joy with your coworkers.

### 188
Have an arts-and-crafts ornament-making afternoon. Lay out a variety of materials at the table, including string or hooks with which to hang the ornaments, and let everyone create their own unique designs.

### 189

Host a silly holiday relay race. Set up the course and then have the players prance like a reindeer, wear a Santa hat over their eyes, or waddle like a penguin. The sillier the race the better.

### 190

Create a fort out of blankets in your living room to watch Christmas movies together. Try and see if you can fill the whole living room with your new hangout spot.

### 191

Watch the Disney Parks Christmas Day Parade televised on ABC on Christmas morning. Check your local TV guide to find out when it airs.

### 192

If you live nearby, visit McAdenville, North Carolina, also known as Christmas Town USA.

### 193

Give back to your community by volunteering at your local food pantry. If you don't have time to volunteer, you can always drop off donations.

### 194

Make a family calendar to give out as a Christmas gift. Gather pictures of your extended family and choose a different photo to go with each month. You can either design the calendar yourself using a word processor or have it professionally made.

# 195
## Make pralines.

### Ingredients
- 1 cup packed dark brown sugar
- 1 cup granulated sugar
- ½ cup evaporated milk
- 1 cup pecan halves or pieces
- 2 tablespoons unsalted butter
- 1½ teaspoons pure vanilla extract

### Directions
- Place the sugars and evaporated milk in a Dutch oven and cook, while stirring constantly, until the sugars have dissolved. Continue cooking, while stirring frequently, until the mixture reaches 225°F.

- Add the pecans and butter, stir until the butter melts, and then remove from heat.

- Stir in the vanilla and let cool while stirring occasionally. When the mixture starts to thicken, place tablespoons of the mixture on a piece of parchment paper. They will settle into thin patties as they cool. Let stand for 30 minutes, then wrap each praline in wax paper.

# 196
# Make chocolate hazelnut dip.

## Ingredients
2 cups hazelnuts
⅓ cup granulated sugar
1 teaspoon sea salt
16 oz. semisweet chocolate, chopped
1 stick of unsalted butter
1 cup heavy whipping cream

## Directions
- Preheat the oven to 350°F. Remove the outer shell from the hazelnuts using a nutcracker.

- Layer the shelled hazelnuts on a baking sheet in one even layer. Roast in the oven for 12 to 15 minutes, then remove and let cool.

- Place the cooled hazelnuts, sugar, and salt into a food processor and blend until the mixture forms a paste.

- Meanwhile, boil ½ inch of water in a saucepan. Set a bowl over the boiling water, making sure the water does not touch the bowl. This is your double boiler. Add the chocolate to the bowl and allow to melt.

- Once melted, remove from heat and whisk in butter and cream. Then, combine the chocolate mixture and the hazelnut paste. Chill before serving.

City sidewalks

Dressed in

In the air there's a

# Busy sidewalks holiday style feeling of Christmas.

—"Silver Bells"

### 197

Have a library trip
where everyone is assigned
another family member. They
have to check out a Christmas
book they think their assigned
family member will like.

### 198

Get the family together
and play Christmas charades.
Be sure to stay on the
holiday theme.

### 199

Set out a Christmas
cracker at everyone's place
at the dinner table. You can
find these during the holiday
season at most mainstream
stores in the US, or make
your own (see page 276).

### 200

Visit your local theater
on a throwback Christmas
movie night.

### 201

Set up a Christmas village.
If you don't already have a
Christmas village collection,
there is no need to run out and
buy one. Challenge yourself
to make one from scratch. You
can even get the kids involved
by using their favorite toys
as different figurines.

### 202

Start the new year
dust-free by doing a deep
clean of your home after the
Christmas decorations
have been put away.

**203**

Have an ongoing Christmas scavenger hunt in the weeks leading up to Christmas. Come up with a list of things to add to your scavenger hunt list such as an outdoor Nativity set, ice skates hanging on someone's door, mistletoe, a snowman, and so on, and give everyone a copy of the list. The first person to see each item gets to cross it off. Whoever has the most points by Christmas Day wins.

**204**

Create calming Christmas glitter jars by mixing festive glitter in water and adding it to a mason jar. To avoid messes, glue the lid shut with a hot glue gun.

**205**

Read the poem "On the Morning of Christ's Nativity" by John Milton.

**206**

If you live nearby, attend the Children's Christmas Parade in Atlanta, Georgia.

**207**

Fight off the winter blues by having a "beach day" in your living room, complete with an umbrella, beach towels, and "water" in the form of a blue blanket. You can even wear bathing suits and watch warm-weather Christmas classics like *The Year Without a Santa Claus* (1974).

# 208
## Make homemade wassail.

### Ingredients
5 apples, cored
¾ cup granulated sugar
8 cups hard cider
½ cup brandy
2 cinnamon sticks
1 tablespoon whole cloves
1 teaspoon nutmeg
1 teaspoon chopped fresh ginger
5 to 6 orange or lemon slices (or a combination)

### Directions
- Heat oven to 350°F. Place apples in a parchment lined baking dish and cover evenly with the sugar. Bake for 30 to 45 minutes or until the apples are soft.

- Meanwhile, combine the cider and brandy in a large pot on the stove and set to medium-low heat. Add the remaining ingredients to the pot and stir gently.

- Once the mixture has heated, strain the liquid into a serving bowl. Add the apples to the bowl, allowing them to float decoratively at the top.

# 209
## Make reindeer noses.

### Ingredients
  1 bag of butter snap pretzels
  1 (12 oz.) bag chocolate candy (such as Rolo's or Hershey's Kisses)
  1 (12 oz.) bag holiday-themed M&Ms

### Directions
- Heat oven to 200°F and cover a large baking sheet with parchment paper. Lay pretzels out on the baking sheet so that they don't overlap (it's okay if the pretzels are touching as long as they are only in one layer).

- Unwrap one piece of candy for every pretzel, and place one piece in the center of each pretzel. Bake in the oven for 4 to 5 minutes, or until the chocolate has just softened.

- Remove tray from the oven and place an M&M in the center of each piece of chocolate, pressing down lightly. Allow to cool fully before eating.

## 210

Make a reverse Advent calendar. Find a large box and divide it into 24 sections. On each day of December, add an item to the box to donate, like canned foods, clothes, or toys. At the end of the month, donate all the items.

## 211

Paint with colored ice cubes. Simply mix washable watercolors and water in an ice tray and freeze overnight, then use them to decorate card stock as they melt.

## 212

Write seasons' greetings as a family using sparklers and the long exposure setting on your camera. This makes a great Christmas card.

## 213

Forego Christmas gifts this year and take that vacation you have been dreaming about. Make sure to choose somewhere that will feel extra magical around the holidays.

## 214

Send Christmas cards over email to conserve resources.

## 215

Look through photo albums or view family slides, movies, or videos with your family.

## 216

Take stock of what you have by writing down one thing you're thankful for each day of December.

## 217

Have a contest at your next holiday gathering to see which team can come up with the corniest plot for a Christmas movie. Give out awards for the "most hilarious," "most terrible," and "most heartwarming" ideas.

## 218

Go head-to-head and see who can make the wildest gingerbread cookies while blindfolded. Make sure to lay down a tablecloth, this can get messy.

## 219

Make a specialty tea box as a gift by selecting a few nice teas and pairing them with a jar of homemade flavored honey (see page 81).

## 220

Purchase handmade Christmas cards from a local artist.

## 221

Make a pomander. Pomanders are pieces of citrus fruit, usually oranges or lemons, that contain cloves in decorative patterns. As the pomander dries out, the juice from the fruit will mix with the scent of the cloves to create a bright, warming aroma. Place pomanders in windows or on shelves to bring some cheer to the dreary winter season.

## 222

Let your kids decorate the windows for the holidays using washable bathtub paints.

# 223

## Serve this delicious café mocha with your Christmas breakfast.

### Ingredients

8 cups whole milk
1 cup heavy cream
½ cup granulated sugar, plus more to taste
½ cup brewed espresso
½ lb. bittersweet chocolate, chopped
1 tablespoon orange zest
½ teaspoon salt
Whipped cream, for garnish

### Directions

· Place the milk, cream, sugar, and espresso in a saucepan and warm over medium heat.

· Place the chocolate in a bowl. When the milk mixture is hot, ladle 1 cup into the bowl containing the chocolate and whisk until the chocolate is completely melted, adding more of the warm milk mixture if the melted chocolate mixture is too thick.

· Pour the melted chocolate mixture into the pot of warm milk and whisk to combine. Add the orange zest and salt, stir to combine, and adjust to taste before topping with the whipped cream.

# 224
# Make flavored honey to give as a gift.

## Ingredients
1 to 2 oz. dried herbs, vegetables, or flowers
1 cup honey

## Directions
- Whatever you choose to infuse the honey with, keep in mind that the smaller the pieces of it are, the more difficult it will be to strain out.

- Place infusing element in the bottom of a jar. Then, fill the jar almost to the top with honey. Using a chopstick or other implement, coat the infusing element with honey. Fill the jar with more honey, then wipe the rim with a clean cloth and cover tightly.

- Let the mixture infuse for at least 5 days. If the infusing element floats to the top, turn the jar over to keep them well coated. For a more intense flavor, infuse for up to 2 weeks.

- Strain the honey into a clean jar. Depending on the volume of the mixture and the size of the strainer, this is best done in stages.

- Secure the jar's lid tightly and store in a cool, dry place. It will last indefinitely.

### 225
Give passes to a local amusement park as Christmas gifts.

### 226
Put on a holiday bazaar for charity. Ask for donated items that could be repurposed as Christmas gifts, and price them affordably so everyone can experience the joy of gift-giving within their budget. Any profits can be donated to the charity of your choice.

### 227
Make ice sculptures by freezing blocks of ice and "carving" them into fun shapes using hot water.

### 228
Make a snow fort.

### 229
Make a shared Spotify playlist and share it with your family so everyone can add their favorite Christmas songs to it.

### 230
Have a stocking guessing game. Fill a Christmas stocking with oddly shaped objects. Have the stocking pass in a circle and let everyone take turns feeling the stocking without peeking. Keep track of everyone's guesses. Whoever gets the most objects right gets to keep the stocking.

### 231

Leave milk and cookies out for Santa. You can even invest in a special mug and plate specifically for Santa.

### 232

If you're traveling to visit family, why not schedule in a few extra days to do some sight-seeing? Christmas is the perfect time to visit a city you've never been to or take a drive through the beautiful snow-covered countryside.

### 233

If you are going to be doing a lot of baking around the holidays, treat yourself to a new piece of equipment like a nice set of baking sheets or a new pie pan.

### 234

Go snowshoeing together.

### 235

Think toward summer with your Christmas gifts this year. A new beach towel or an inflatable pool may not be practical for winter but thinking of using them come summertime will help everyone through the long winter.

### 236

Keep track of how many ornaments are on your Christmas tree. At your next Christmas party, have guests guess the number of ornaments. The closest guess wins.

# 237
## Make a cream puff cake.

### Ingredients
  1 stick of unsalted butter
  1 cup water
  1 cup all-purpose flour
  4 eggs
  Premade pastry cream

### Directions
- Preheat the oven to 375°F and grease a Bundt pan with nonstick cooking spray.

- Place the butter and water in a large saucepan and bring to a boil over medium-high heat.

- Reduce the heat to low and add the flour. Cook, while stirring, until the mixture forms a ball and pulls away from the edges of the pan. Remove from heat.

- Add the eggs one at a time, beating to incorporate each one before adding the next.

- Transfer the mixture to the prepared Bundt pan, place in the oven, and bake until golden brown and a knife inserted into the center comes out clean, about 40 to 45 minutes. Remove and allow the cake to cool completely.

- Invert the cooled cake onto a plate. Slice the cake in half along the equator. Spread the pastry cream over the bottom layer, replace the top layer, and serve.

# 238
## Bake a pumpkin ginger loaf.

### Ingredients

1½ cups all-purpose flour, plus more for dusting
¼ teaspoon salt
1 teaspoon baking powder
½ teaspoon baking soda
1 tablespoon candied ginger, finely chopped
1 teaspoon ground cinnamon
Pinch of cloves
¾ cup packed dark brown sugar
1 cup canned pumpkin puree
½ cup sunflower oil
2 eggs

### Directions

- Preheat the oven to 350°F. Sift together the flour, salt, baking powder, baking soda, and dry spices.

- In a large bowl, mix together the sugar, pumpkin, oil, and eggs. Pour the wet ingredients into the dry and gently stir together until incorporated.

- Pour the batter into a greased and floured loaf pan. Bake for 50 to 60 minutes or until a toothpick comes out clean.

## 239

Listen to classic Christmas music.

## 240

Pay attention to your winter landscaping. Gardening might seem like a summer job, but you can make sure your yard remains beautiful all through the winter by utilizing winter plants, lighting fixtures, and natural decorations to make your yard a focal point all year long.

## 241

Make Christmas decorations using old holiday cards. You can cut them into a garland or create disks of different sizes and arrange them on a wooden dowel to make a mini Christmas tree.

## 242

Have a stay-up-late night over Christmas vacation where the kids can stay up as late as they want (within reason) and just spend time together as a family.

## 243

Play human wreath. Get everyone together in a circle and have them join hands with two people across the middle of the circle. Once everyone has linked hands, the goal is to untangle the human wreath without letting go of anyone's hands. This requires real teamwork, so be sure to take your time and help younger players. Once you're all standing in a circle with your hands untangled, you've won!

**244**

Have your kids make or choose personalized Christmas gifts for their teachers, daycare staff, or babysitters. Some ideas include hand-painted coffee mugs, a handmade ornament, or a gift certificate to a local coffee shop.

**245**

Have a Christmas song naming contest. Break off into two to three teams. You can either have someone play the first few seconds of a Christmas song, or you can sing the first verse. Whoever can name the Christmas song first, wins. Looking for an extra challenge? Award bonus points for guessing the album and artist, too.

**246**

Tie Christmas ribbons around the trees in your yard.

**247**

Play the name game but with favorite Christmas traditions to see how well you know your family. Simply create a circle of family members and pass a ball back and forth. Before passing the ball to someone, however, you have to yell something they like about Christmas. See how fast you can get the ball going!

**248**

Have a sword fight using wrapping paper tubes.

# The Christmas
# spirit of giving

spirit is a
and forgiving.

—James Cash Penney

# 249

# Make peppermint bark brownies.

## Ingredients

6 oz. semisweet chocolate chips
1 stick of unsalted butter, cut into tablespoons
2 large eggs
1 cup granulated sugar
1 teaspoon vanilla extract
1 cup flour
½ teaspoon baking powder
Pinch of salt
1 cup peppermint bark pieces, chopped small

## Directions

· Preheat the oven to 350°F. Lightly grease an 8 x 8-inch baking dish.

· In a double boiler, melt the chocolate chips and butter together slowly, stirring constantly. Transfer the mixture to a large bowl. Stir in the eggs, sugar, and vanilla. In the measuring cup with the flour, mix in the baking powder and pinch of salt. Add the flour mixture to the chocolate, stirring to blend well.

· Pour the batter into the baking dish. Sprinkle the peppermint bark evenly over the top of the brownies. Bake for about 30 minutes, until a knife inserted in the middle comes out clean. Be careful not to overcook. Allow to cool for 20 to 30 minutes before serving.

# 250
## Make Polish chrusciki.

### Ingredients
  3 large eggs, at room temperature
  ¼ cup whole milk
  ¾ cup granulated sugar
  1 stick of unsalted butter
  1 teaspoon baking soda
  1 teaspoon vanilla extract
  ½ teaspoon salt
  ½ teaspoon grated nutmeg
  3½ cups all-purpose flour, plus more for dusting
  Vegetable oil, for frying
  1 cup confectioners' sugar, for dusting

### Directions
- Combine the eggs, milk, granulated sugar, and butter in a mixing bowl and whisk until well combined. Whisk in the baking soda, vanilla, salt, and nutmeg, and then add the flour. Mix until a soft dough forms, cover the bowl tightly, and chill in the refrigerator for 1 hour.

- Dust a work surface and rolling pin with flour. Roll out the dough to an even thickness of ¼ inch. Cut dough into 1-inch-wide strips. Cut strips on a diagonal at 3-inch intervals to form diamond-shaped cookies.

- Pour 1½ inches of oil in a deep Dutch oven. Heat to 375°F and add the cookies a few at a time, using a slotted spoon to turn them as they brown. When the cookies are browned all over, remove, set to drain on paper towels, and sprinkle with confectioners' sugar. Serve immediately.

### 251

If you go out to eat during the holidays, leave an extra-large tip as a Christmas surprise for your server.

### 252

Make an Advent calendar paperchain. Start on the first day of December and attach a link every day. By Christmas you will have a finished festive chain.

### 253

Make pancake shapes for Christmas morning by placing pancake batter and food coloring in squeeze bottles and using them to make cool designs. This can take some practice, but the results are worth the effort.

### 254

Watch *Noelle* (2019).

### 255

Decorate your Christmas tree using only recycled materials this year. You can make homemade ornaments and swap out tinsel for shredded tin foil or magazine pages.

### 256

Take a Christmas road trip.

### 257

Have a Christmas Eve campout in your living room. You can set up a tent, read Christmas stories by flashlight, and even eat marshmallows while you wait for Santa.

## 258
Decorate your car for
Christmas with press-on
Christmas window decals.

## 259
Make your own traditional
Advent calendar complete
with chocolates and
small gifts.

## 260
Go bowling as a family.
You can make it even more
festive by dressing up
in ugly sweaters.

## 261
Have a pancake bar
breakfast, complete with fun
toppings like berries, whipped
cream, and chocolate chips.

## 262
Make marshmallow
constellations using licorice
to connect the dots.

## 263
Listen to
"I Want a Hippopotamus
for Christmas" by
Gayla Peevey.

## 264
Make a Christmas
wreath using wrapped
chocolate balls. Simply glue
wrapped chocolates to a
circular piece of cardboard.
As people eat the chocolates
throughout the holidays,
the wrappers left behind
will make a fun and
vibrant wreath.

# 265
# Make an elegant plum galette.

### Ingredients

1 ball of premade pie dough
All-purpose flour, for dusting
3 cups pitted and sliced plums
½ cup granulated sugar, plus 1 tablespoon
Juice of ½ lemon
3 tablespoons cornstarch
Pinch of salt
2 tablespoons blackberry jam
1 egg, beaten

### Directions

· Preheat the oven to 400°F. Place the ball of dough on a flour-dusted work surface, roll it out to 9 inches, and place it on a parchment-lined baking sheet.

· Place the plums, the ½ cup of sugar, lemon juice, cornstarch, and salt in a mixing bowl and stir until the plums are evenly coated.

· Spread the jam over the crust, making sure to leave 1½ inches of dough around the edge. Place the filling on top of the jam and fold the crust over it. Brush the crust with the beaten egg and sprinkle it with the remaining sugar.

· Put the galette in the oven and bake until the crust is golden brown and the filling is bubbly, about 35 to 40 minutes. Remove from the oven and allow to cool before serving.

# 266
# Make mason jar candle holders.

## Tools
Scissors
Waxed paper
Mason jars with lid rims
Double-sided tape
Paint of choice
LED votive candles

## Directions
- Cut a Christmas shape out of the waxed paper, like a Christmas tree or star. Then, tape this shape to the mason jar using double-sided tape. Be sure all edges are taped down.

- Paint the outside of the mason jar with your paint of choice, painting around the waxed paper. Once the paint dries, remove the waxed paper to reveal the Christmas shape.

- Place the rim of the mason jar lid around the top, leaving the center of the lid open. Add a votive candle and enjoy the festive light display.

## 267
Watch *The Little Drummer Boy* (1968).

## 268
If you go out to eat with friends this holiday season, pick up the tab as a Christmas surprise.

## 269
Challenge yourself to finish all your Christmas shopping in one day so you can relax and enjoy the rest of the season without worrying about getting everything done.

## 270
Watch *Olive, the Other Reindeer* (1999).

## 271
Put on your own Christmas pageant.

## 272
Make a no-sew blanket using two pieces of Christmas-themed fleece fabric. Cut into each side, making strips that are about 1 inch wide and 4 inches long but are still attached at the center of the fabric. Then, tie the edges of the pieces of fabric together to make your new blanket.

## 273
Make gift baskets for your local retirement community or hospital.

**274**
Watch *Arthur Christmas* (2011).

**275**
Make your own tea bags. Get some resealable tea sachets and fill them with your favorite ingredients, like lemongrass and dried ginger. These make great Christmas gifts.

**276**
Bring your loved ones cups of hot chocolate in bed on Christmas morning.

**277**
Do a Christmas word search.

**278**
Read *Christmas in Noisy Village* by Astrid Lindgren.

**279**
Set up a pretend hot cocoa shop in the living room (with real hot cocoa, of course).

**280**
Watch different movie adaptions of Charles Dickens's *A Christmas Carol* and have your family vote on their favorite. Here are a few good versions to check out: *Scrooge* (1970), *The Muppet Christmas Carol* (1992), *Disney's A Christmas Carol* (2009).

# 281
## Serve this Dutch apple baby at a Christmas party.

### Ingredients
- 2 tart apples, cored, peeled, and sliced
- 4 tablespoons unsalted butter
- ¼ cup granulated sugar, plus 3 tablespoons
- 1 tablespoon cinnamon
- ¾ cup flour
- ¼ teaspoon salt
- ¾ cup milk
- 4 eggs
- 1 teaspoon vanilla or almond extract
- Confectioners' sugar, for dusting

## Directions

- Preheat the oven to 425°F and position a rack in the center. Heat a cast-iron skillet over medium-high heat. Add the apples and butter and cook, while stirring, until the apples soften, about 3 to 4 minutes. Add the ¼ cup of sugar and the cinnamon and cook for another 3 or 4 minutes. Distribute the apples evenly over the bottom of the skillet and remove from heat.

- In a large bowl, mix the remaining sugar, flour, and salt together. In a smaller bowl, whisk together the milk, eggs, and vanilla or almond extract. Add the wet mixture and the dry mixture and stir to combine. Pour the resulting batter over the apples.

- Put the skillet in the oven and bake for 15 to 20 minutes until puffy and browned on top. Remove the skillet from the oven and let cool for a few minutes. Run a knife along the edge of the skillet to loosen the dessert and then put a plate over the skillet. Using oven mitts or potholders, flip the skillet over so the dessert transfers to the plate. Dust with confectioners' sugar and serve warm.

### 182
Watch *While You Were Sleeping* (1995).

### 183
Make toilet paper roll snowmen using white paint, markers, and scraps of paper for the scarf and hat. You can use toothpicks for the arms, if you'd like.

### 184
Glue a loop of decorative string to the end of a piece of ribbon candy to turn it into a festive ornament.

### 185
Make toilet paper roll reindeer using pipe cleaners for the legs and antlers.

### 186
Use a Christmas-themed fabric loosely wrapped around the tree as an affordable alternative to a Christmas tree skirt.

### 187
Prepare table gifts for your Christmas dinner. When you set the table, place a small, wrapped gift at every place setting. They can be random gifts or labeled for a specific person. Old fashioned wooden toys are fun for children, and for adults small boxes of chocolates or classic books are nice options.

### 188
Read *The Twelve Days of Christmas* by Alison Jay.

### 289
If you put out a pitcher of water on your Christmas dinner table, add cranberries to it to make it look more festive.

### 290
Offer to help elderly friends or neighbors do their Christmas shopping or wrapping.

### 291
Grow a rosemary plant indoors. You can find rosemary plants pruned to look like miniature Christmas trees around the holidays.

### 292
Get up early on Christmas morning and watch the sunrise from a scenic place.

### 293
Read "The Gift of the Magi" by O. Henry.

### 294
Any little ones in your life will want to be sure that Santa can easily find your house on Christmas Eve. Make things easy on him by lining your driveway with landing lights. Place LED votive candles inside small brown paper lunch bags and line them on either side of your street or driveway to make a nice spot for Santa to land.

### 295
Try sourcing as many ingredients as possible from local farmers or businesses for your Christmas dinner.

# 296
# Make a tissue paper candle votive.

## Tools
    Recycled clear glass jar
    Mod Podge
    Tissue paper cut into randomly shaped pieces (about 1 to 2 square inches)
    Thick paint brush
    LED or wax tea light
    Ribbon or string, for decoration (optional)

## Directions
- Begin by thoroughly washing and drying your glass container of choice. Spread Mod Podge on a small section of the jar and attach a piece of tissue paper. Allow to dry slightly before painting glue over the top and attaching the next piece. Allow each piece of paper to overlap slightly. Continue gluing until the entire outside of the jar is covered.

- Allow to dry fully before placing a tea light inside and lighting.

# 297
## Make chow mein noodle cookies.

### Ingredients
1 cup chocolate chips
1 cup butterscotch chips
1 teaspoon vegetable shortening
1 (5 oz.) can chow mein noodles
½ cup red and green M&Ms

### Directions
- Begin by pouring chocolate chips and butterscotch chips into a large microwavable bowl. Add the shortening and stir lightly. Microwave in 30 second intervals until the chips have melted.

- In a large bowl, pour the chow mein noodles and M&Ms and stir. Pour the melted chocolate over the noodle mixture and stir with a fork until all the noodles and M&Ms are coated.

- Using two forks or your hands, gather the noodles into small clusters and place them on a sheet of wax paper. Allow the chocolate to harden completely before serving.

May you grown up to skies on

never be too
search the
Christmas Eve.

—Unknown

## 298
Go ice fishing.

## 299
Promote shopping local by having a handmade-only white elephant gift exchange! Either buy from a local artisan or try crafting something yourself.

## 300
If your kids have a favorite stuffed animal, get them their own miniature Christmas tree that they can decorate, complete with small lights. Set this next to your normal tree and add small presents addressed to the stuffy from Santa for a nice Christmas morning surprise.

## 301
Who says Christmas cookies have to be shaped like mittens and snowflakes? Look for something unique like zombie or Star Wars cookie cutters to spice up your seasonal snacks.

## 302
Have a Christmas-themed face painting night.

## 303
If you don't feel like making dessert on Christmas, order something special from a bakery in advance.

## 304
Give your family pet a new bed in time for Christmas Eve.

### 305

Give someone the gift
of life by donating blood
near the holidays.

### 306

Decorate the ultimate ugly
Christmas sweater together
and then have a fashion show.
You can use fabric paints,
glitter, ornaments, pipe
cleaners, and anything else
that strikes your fancy.

### 307

Send fresh fruit as a
gift. Many websites offer
high-quality specialty fruit like
pears, oranges, or grapefruits
that can be sent to family and
friends. The perfect gift for
those trying to avoid sweets
around the holidays.

### 308

Bake your favorite
bread recipe together.
Be sure to enjoy it warm
with plenty of butter
or jam.

### 309

Save up postcards
from your family vacation
and send them out instead
of Christmas cards.

### 310

Make animated
holiday flipbooks out of
sticky notes by starting a
drawing at one corner of the
pad of notes, and then having
it move on each subsequent
note. Flip the edges of the
pad to see your figure
in action.

# 311
# Make almond meringues as Christmas gifts.

Ingredients
- Whites of 4 large eggs
- ½ teaspoon pure almond extract
- Pinch of salt
- 2 teaspoons cornstarch
- ¾ cup granulated sugar
- ⅓ cup chopped almonds, toasted

### Directions

- Preheat the oven to 225°F and line two baking sheets with parchment paper. As timing is crucial, place a piping bag near your workstation and fit the stand mixer with the whisk attachment.

- Place the egg whites, almond extract, and salt in the mixing bowl of the stand mixer and beat on high until soft peaks form.

- Add the cornstarch and sugar, reduce the speed to medium, and beat until incorporated. Raise speed to high and beat until stiff peaks start to form. Transfer the mixture to your piping bag and pipe onto the parchment-lined baking sheets. Sprinkle with the toasted almonds, place on separate racks in the oven and bake for 1 hour, while rotating the baking sheets halfway through. Turn off the oven, leave the meringues in the oven, and let them cool for another hour.

- Remove from the oven and let cool to room temperature before serving.

**Tip:** If you do not have a piping bag, simply fill a large resealable bag with the mixture, cut off one of the corners, and squeeze.

### 312

Make a popcorn and cranberry garland. Thread a needle with a long piece of heavy-duty thread (about two yards) leaving a two-inch tail. Make a large, sturdy knot on the long end of the thread. Begin threading pieces of popped, unbuttered popcorn and whole, fresh cranberries onto the thread. You can alternate one piece of popcorn with one cranberry or form your own patterns.

### 313

Crochet or knit a set of simple potholders, washcloths, or coasters as a Christmas gift. You can elevate the Christmas cheer by alternating red and green yarn.

### 314

Visit a family member at work if they have to go in on Christmas Eve or Christmas Day.

### 315

Frost the windows using spray snow.

### 316

Listen to *Christmas With The Chipmunks* by Alvin & The Chipmunks.

### 317

Wrap sprigs of pine and bittersweet into bushels, tie with twine, and hang them from the ceiling in your home.

### 318
Watch *Silent Night* (2002).

### 319
Write and illustrate your own Christmas story as a family.

### 320
Make gingerbread paper dolls. Trace a gingerbread cutter on brown construction paper and cut it out. Cut out "candy" pieces from other colored paper and use them to decorate the gingerbread figure. Then, hang up around your house to spread the Christmas spirit.

### 321
Go to an escape room while everyone is home for the holidays.

### 322
Make a holiday time capsule. You can include drawings, pictures, letters to your future selves, or anything else you want. Then, bury the time capsule or hide it away in your house and open it the following Christmas

### 323
Have a pillow fight together. Just watch out for the Christmas tree.

### 324
Go for a walk in the woods at sunset and enjoy the light on the snow.

### 325
Watch *The Night Before Christmas* (2015).

# 326
# Make traditional hot cross buns.

## Ingredients
### For the Buns
½ cup water
1 tablespoon active dry yeast
¾ cup milk
4½ cups all-purpose flour
⅓ cup granulated sugar
2 eggs
3½ tablespoons unsalted butter
1¾ teaspoons salt
⅔ cup raisins
1 cup chopped, candied orange or lemon peels
1 apple, peeled, cored, and finely chopped
Zest of 1 orange
1 teaspoon ground cinnamon

### For the Cross
¾ cups all-purpose flour
½ cup water

### For the Glaze
Apricot jam

## Directions

- Heat the water to 100°F to 110°F. Dissolve the yeast in the water and let rest for 5 minutes. In a large bowl, combine the water-yeast mixture with the warmed milk, ½ of the flour, and the sugar. Add one egg at a time and incorporate well. Add the rest of the flour and start working the dough, either with a stand-mixer or by hand.

- Add the butter in pieces, continuing to work the dough, and incorporate the salt towards the end of the kneading. Work the dough until it feels smooth. The mixing process takes about 20 minutes from start to finish.

- Let the dough rest, covered, in a warm spot until it looks fully risen, about 1 to 2 hours. Transfer the dough to a clean surface. Incorporate all other ingredients, folding them in until evenly distributed.

- Divide the dough into 12 to 15 pieces of about ¾ to 1 cup each. Roll into small rounds and place on one or two baking trays covered with parchment paper. Cover with an oiled plastic film or place into a large plastic bag and let rest for about 1 to 1½ hours.

- Preheat oven to 425°F. Prepare the finish for the cross by combining the flour with the water and filling a piping bag with it. Decorate the top of each bun by piping a cross over it. Bake for 20 to 25 minutes. Glaze while still warm with warmed apricot jam.

### 327

Have a gift wrap relay.
Divide into two teams and see
who can wrap presents the
fastest. Be sure to award points
for speed, accuracy, and style.

### 328

Hang tinsel on your
Christmas tree for an extra
touch of sparkle.

### 329

Do your Christmas
shopping at stores that make
a point to donate part of their
proceeds to charity.

### 330

Read *Christmas in the
Big Woods* by Laura
Ingalls Wilder.

### 331

Have a crazy Christmas
hairdo contest. Hang
ornaments from your hair,
braid in tinsel, or use hair
glitter—the crazier the better.

### 332

Grow paperwhites.
These delicate white
flowers are in the daffodil
family and will make a delicate
and beautiful centerpiece for
your Christmas table. You
can also purchase fully-grown
plants locally for an instant
holiday decoration.

### 333

Read *The World
Encyclopedia of Christmas*
by Gerry Bowler.

### 334

Have a group sing-along to "The Twelve Days of Christmas." To do this you will need about twelve people, but if you have fewer than twelve multiple people can share a verse. Assign each person one of the gifts that the speaker receives in the song. Whenever a gift is mentioned in the song, that person sings their part alone, and then everyone else joins in on the rest of the song. This can take some practice to pull off, but the results are worth it.

### 335

Bring all of your kids to the dollar store and let them pick out one present for each member of your family.

### 336

Watch *The Nightmare Before Christmas* (1993).

### 337

Take a few private moments to be grateful for all that you have this Christmas.

### 338

Wear your pajamas as many days as possible during Christmas vacation.

### 339

Gift each member of your family a new set of Christmas sheets.

### 340

Read *Eloise at Christmastime* by Rachel Isadora.

# 341
## Make a sock snowman.

### Tools
- 1 white cotton tube sock
- 3 cups beans or rice
- 2 rubber bands
- Hot glue gun
- 1 ribbon or strip of fabric, for a scarf
- Pom-poms and googly eyes, for the face
- Additional decorations of choice

### Directions
- Begin by turning the sock inside out (so the fuzzy part of the sock is exposed) and fill it with rice or beans up to the base of the ankle (do not overfill or you won't be able to divide the snowman at the middle.

- Twist the sock closed at the ankle and tie with a rubber band. Cut off the remaining, unfilled piece of the sock.

- Twist the sock ⅔ of the way from the cut end to create two sections (one smaller section for the head, and a larger section for the body). Attach rubber band to hold.

- Use the glue gun to decorate the snowman, giving it a scarf, face, or any other desired decorations.

# 342
## Make baked stuffed apples.

### Ingredients
    6 pink lady apples
    3 tablespoons unsalted butter, melted
    6 tablespoons blackberry jam
    2 oz. goat cheese, cut into 6 rounds

### Directions
· Preheat the oven to 350°F. Slice the tops off the apples and set aside. Use a paring knife to cut a circle around the apples' cores and then scoop out the centers. Make sure to leave a ½-inch thick wall inside the apple.

· Rub the inside and outside of the apples with some of the melted butter. Place the jam and goat cheese in a mixing bowl and stir to combine. Fill the apples' cavities with the mixture, place the tops back on the apples, and set them aside.

· Warm a cast-iron skillet over medium-high heat. Add the remaining butter, place the apples in the skillet, and place the skillet in the oven. Bake until tender, 25 to 30 minutes. Remove from the oven and let cool briefly before serving.

## 343

Label all of your Christmas decorations with their names in another language you want to learn.

## 344

Visit a town you've never been to before and check out their Christmas celebrations.

## 345

Give your Christmas tree a theme and only use decorations to fit that theme. You can go with natural themes or go for nerdy themes like Harry Potter or Star Wars.

## 346

Read *A Charlie Brown Christmas* by Charles M. Schulz.

## 347

Play the related words game. Going in a circle, have one person come up with a holiday word. The next person has three seconds to come up with a related word before they are out. Remember, no repeats!

## 348

Start a coat drive for a local homeless shelter or charity.

## 349

Learn string games like cat's cradle and play them together for a fun, unplugged activity for cold winter nights.

## 350

Make a donation to a local hospital.

### 351
Add Christmas M&Ms to your popcorn for a sweet kick.

### 352
Have a Grinch marathon by watching *How the Grinch Stole Christmas!* (1966), *How the Grinch Stole Christmas* (2000), and *Dr. Seuss' The Grinch* (2018) all in one day or on three consecutive nights.

### 353
Make a Diet Coke and Mentos eruption in the snow. You can even build "volcanoes" around the bottles for added effect.

### 354
Read the poem "The Oxen" by Thomas Hardy.

### 355
Attend a performance of Handel's "Messiah."

### 356
Go on an ugly sweater scavenger hunt at your local thrift store. Come up with a list of classic ugly sweater designs and have each person try and see how many they can find. The winner gets to buy the ugliest Christmas sweater from the lot.

### 357
Turn a not-so-fun job into a family project by getting everyone involved in the outdoor decoration process. The task will go by quicker and you'll make memories while you're at it.

Seeing is believing, most real things the things

but sometimes the
in the world are
we can't see.

—*The Polar Express* (2004)

# 358
# Play Christmas would you rather.

**How to play:**

- Have one person be the question asker. The rest of the family gathers in the center of the room. Designate one side of the room as one answer to the question, and the other side of the room as the second answer.

- The question asker asks the group to choose between two options, like choosing between candy canes and hot cocoa, and each person runs to the side they would rather pick. They then explain why they picked that option to the group. Remember: there's no sitting down in the center of the room if you can't decide.

# 359
## Play naughty or nice.

**How to play:**

- Each player goes around the circle and asks another player to pick between "naughty" or "nice." If they choose "nice," the player gets to ask them a question of their choice, though you should try and stay on a holiday theme.

- If they refuse to answer the question or choose "naughty," the player can choose to have them do something ridiculous, like wear a candy cane on their head for the rest of the night or sing a Christmas carol on video. If they refuse, they're out of the game. The game ends when there is only one player left in the circle.

## 360
Grow a poinsettia.
You can find these festive holiday plants already potted around Christmas time, just make sure not to buy them if you have cats or dogs; they are poisonous to many animals.

## 361
Make a tray with a tea pot and mugs to bring into the living room on Christmas morning while you open gifts.

## 362
Give each of your kids a new snow shovel for Christmas to encourage them to help out with the shoveling this winter.

## 363
Play the chocolate description game. First, get a box of chocolates. If the box comes with a description of each chocolate, have each player blindly choose a random chocolate to taste. The taster then tries to describe the chocolate to the best of their ability. The person whose description most closely matches the one in the box, wins.

## 364
Give everyone a calendar for Christmas to use in the new year.

## 365
Wear your pajamas all day long on Christmas Day.

## 366
Cover your dining table with craft paper and paint a giant collaborative Christmas mural.

## 367
Attend a Christmas service at your local church of choice.

## 368
Pay attention to what you eat in the weeks and days leading up to Christmas. A whole month of healthy eating will make your Christmas treats much sweeter.

## 369
Give an amaryllis bulb as a gift. Or you can save the recipient some work by potting the bulb yourself and including care instructions.

## 370
Put a giant bow on your front door.

## 371
Draw a picture blindfolded (make sure to stay on the holiday theme). Have the rest of your family silently guess what you drew and draw their own version of it without a blindfold. Once they all draw their answers, tell them what you drew and see what everyone came up with!

## 372
Host a bake sale for charity. You know you're already going to be in the kitchen at the holidays, so why not make a few extra treats for a good cause?

# 373
## Play deck the halls.

**Tools**
 Plastic ornaments
 Tinsel
 Decorative strings
 Any other holiday decorations

**How to play:**
- In this game, one player gets to be the Christmas tree of their dreams. Splitting up into teams of two or more, each team's goal is to decorate their "Christmas tree" the fastest using all the decorations provided. The player being decorated cannot help in any way at all, other than verbal instructions. Whoever completes their Christmas tree first, wins.

# 374
## Make Sleek Heat Sangria.

### Ingredients
**For the Ginger Simple Syrup**
    1 cup granulated sugar
    1 cup water
    1 piece fresh ginger root, peeled and sliced thin

**For the Sangria**
    1 bottle (750ml) dry white wine
    1 cup seedless green grapes, halved and frozen
    2 plums, pitted and cut into bite-sized pieces, frozen
    1 cup seltzer

### Directions
- To make the Ginger Simple Syrup, in a small saucepan combine the sugar and water. Cook over medium heat, while stirring, until sugar is dissolved. Add the fresh ginger slices. Remove from the heat and cover, letting the ginger steep for about 2 hours.

- Remove the slices and strain the syrup into a jar to remove any pulp. Cover and refrigerate. The syrup will keep in the refrigerator, tightly sealed, for up to 2 weeks.

- To make the sangria, combine ½ cup Ginger Simple Syrup with all ingredients except the seltzer in a large pitcher or container. Cover and refrigerate for 4 or more hours. Add ice and seltzer. Stir and serve.

**375**

Visit a zoo near you that stays open in the winter.

**376**

Make an ice bowling set by freezing water in a balloon and milk cartons for the bowling ball and pins. Feel free to add glitter or other festive decorations if you so choose.

**377**

Drive to a scenic overlook and watch the stars on a cold winter night. Be sure to bring plenty of blankets and hot cocoa.

**378**

If you live nearby, attend the Mayor's Annual Christmas parade in Baltimore, Maryland.

**379**

Make peppermint bark dip. In a medium bowl, beat 4 oz. softened cream cheese until it's light and fluffy. Stir in 3 cups whipped cream until completely incorporated. Add ¼ cup peppermint bark pieces and ⅓ cup chocolate chips and stir to combine. Transfer to a bowl and put it in the middle of a plate with different cookies all around to serve.

**380**

Watch *Krampus* (2015) for a scary twist in your Christmas movie line-up.

### 381

Remember that friend
you lost touch with years ago?
Send them a Christmas card
this holiday season.

### 382

Create a family holiday
workout routine. This is a
great way to keep each
other on track during the
Christmas season.

### 383

Donate money to a good
cause in someone's name.

### 384

Keep a set of special
dishes that you only use on
Christmas. They don't have to
be fancy to become a beloved
Christmas tradition!

### 385

Give a family member
who likes to cook a "cooking
basket." Go to your local
kitchen store and put together
a collection of essentials like
an apron, baking sheets,
and spatulas.

### 386

Make a gingerbread
replica of your house using
the gingerbread recipe
on page 20.

### 387

Have a "blind date"
with a book by wrapping your
favorite books in Christmas
wrapping paper and then
randomly choosing one
to read out loud.

# 388
## Make peanut butter and jam thumbprint cookies.

### Ingredients
¾ cup packed light brown sugar
1 stick of unsalted butter, at room temperature
1 cup creamy peanut butter
1 large egg, at room temperature
½ teaspoon pure vanilla extract
1 teaspoon baking soda
⅛ teaspoon salt
1 cup all-purpose flour
1½ cups seedless raspberry jam

## Directions

- Preheat the oven to 375°F and line two baking sheets with parchment paper. Combine the brown sugar, butter, and peanut butter in the mixing bowl of a stand mixer and beat at low speed until combined. Increase the speed to high and beat until the mixture is light and fluffy.

- Add the egg, vanilla, baking soda, and salt and beat for 1 minute. Slowly add the flour and beat until a soft dough forms.

- Remove tablespoons of the dough and roll them into balls. Place the balls on the baking sheets, 1½ inches apart. Use your index finger to make a large depression in the center of each ball. Place the cookies into the oven and bake for 10 to 12 minutes, until the edges are brown. Remove, let cool for 2 minutes, and then transfer to wire racks to cool completely.

- While the cookies are cooling, place the raspberry jam in a saucepan and cook over medium heat. Bring to a boil, while stirring frequently, and cook until the jam has been reduced by one-quarter. Spoon a teaspoon of the jam into each cookie and allow it to set.

**389**
Have a snowman
building contest.

**390**
Take an evening to drive
around town looking at all
the Christmas lights and have
everyone vote on their favorite
display. Don't forget to pack a
thermos of hot chocolate.

**391**
Have a stocking relay.
Fill two bowls with wrapped
holiday candy and set two
stockings across the room
from the bowls. Each team is
given a spoon and has to fill
the stocking with all of the
candy in the bowl as fast as
possible. The first group to
get all their candy in the
stocking, wins.

**392**
Write letters
to Santa together.

**393**
Set a goal to spend at least an
hour of family time together
each day during the holidays.

**394**
Give a set of Christmas
coasters to a friend
for Christmas.

**395**
Give passes to a local museum
as Christmas gifts.

**396**
Have a breakfast-in-bed
rotation during the holidays.
Each day another person gets
to be the one being served.

### 397
Have everyone pick
out new slippers to wear on
Christmas morning.

### 398
At Christmas dinner, have
each family member go
around the table and share one
important thing that they have
learned in the past year.

### 399
Have a light party on the
Winter Solstice. You can light
candles, hang lights, enjoy
bright-themed foods, and
celebrate togetherness on the
longest night of the year.

### 400
Attend a performance
of Disney on Ice.

### 401
Turn your hallway
into a magical winter
wonderland by hanging
icicle lights from the ceiling
using adhesive hooks.

### 402
Let your kids decorate the
inside of your car with
garlands, ornaments, and
more. Just be sure not to
obscure any windows.

### 403
Have a cookie day.
Set aside an entire day just
for baking Christmas cookies.
Try making an assortment of
cookies, and when you're done,
you can package them up and
deliver them to friends
and neighbors.

# 404
# Make barked-up peppermint pinwheel cookies.

## Ingredients
1¼ cups flour
¾ teaspoon baking powder
¼ teaspoon salt
1 stick of unsalted butter, at room temperature
¾ cup granulated sugar
1 egg
½ teaspoon vanilla
½ teaspoon peppermint extract
3 to 5 drops red food coloring
1 cup peppermint bark, broken into small pieces

## Directions
- In a medium bowl, whisk together the flour, baking powder, and salt. Set aside.

- In a large bowl, beat together the butter and sugar with an electric beater or by hand until the mixture is light and fluffy. Beat in the egg until thoroughly combined, and then add the vanilla.

- On low speed or with a large spoon, stir the flour mixture into the butter-and-sugar mixture, working with about ½ cup flour at a time and beating or stirring until thoroughly combined.

- Divide the dough in half. To prevent staining, put one half in a glass or stainless-steel bowl and add the peppermint extract and food coloring. Stir to combine thoroughly.

- Wrap each dough in plastic wrap, flattening out the dough into a small square or rectangle. Refrigerate for about an hour so the dough is easier to work with.

- On a large flat surface, roll out the plain dough into a rectangle approximately 12 x 6-inches. Transfer to a piece of waxed paper. Repeat with the red dough, and place this on top of the other dough. Starting with a long end, roll the dough into a log, peeling off the waxed paper as you do.

- When the log is formed, wrap in plenty of plastic wrap and refrigerate again until firm, at least 4 hours or up to 2 days. Preheat the oven to 350°F. Line a baking sheet with parchment paper.

- Unwrap the cookie dough and slice into ¼-inch thick rounds. Position on the cookie sheet and sprinkle with pieces of peppermint bark. Bake for 12 to 15 minutes, until the edges are browned. Transfer to a wire rack to cool.

Oh the weather
But the fire is
And since we've
Let it snow, let it

outside is frightful,
so delightful,
no place to go,
snow, let it snow.

—"Let It Snow"

### 405
Host a natural decorating party in your home. Gather a few friends and some natural materials like pine branches, bittersweet, pinecones, and dried fruit and see what festive decorations you can create.

### 406
Paint Christmas-themed pottery at a ceramic painting studio and give them as gifts.

### 407
Watch *The Santa Clause 2* (2002).

### 408
Play outdoor tic-tac-toe in the snow using squirt bottles filled with food coloring and water.

### 409
Wear a Christmas-themed tie or hairbow to work on Christmas Eve.

### 410
Burn a holiday scented candle.

### 411
Have a Christmas movie scavenger hunt. This works especially well with made-for-TV movies. Make up a list of Christmas movie tropes and hand them out to each family member. Whoever spots each trope first gets to cross it off their list. You can include fun options like, "The spirit of Christmas saves the day" or, "Everyone sings a Christmas carol."

### 412

Mix up your white elephant gift exchange by playing with two decks of cards. Each player brings a wrapped gift and places it in the center of the room. Shuffle two decks of cards and divide one deck evenly among the players. Draw cards from the second deck, and when a card is pulled, the player who has the matching card in their hand will choose a gift to unwrap and decide if they will keep or swap for a gift that has already been opened. This method gives everyone the chance to swap gifts multiple times. The person with the last card to be drawn from the deck gets their pick of all the gifts with no risk of having it stolen.

### 413

Watch *Home Alone 2: Lost in New York* (1992).

### 414

Start a Christmas tradition of going for a walk in a beautiful place on Christmas Eve. This can be a nice, refreshing getaway from the stress of the holidays.

### 415

Have a Christmas morning picnic. If you live somewhere colder, you can always lay out a picnic blanket in the living room and enjoy breakfast by the Christmas tree.

### 416

Read *Christmas Day in the Morning* by Pearl S. Buck.

# 417
## Make Yankee short ribs with roasted potatoes and carrots for Christmas dinner.

### Ingredients
2 tablespoons canola oil
4 lbs. bone-in short ribs
Salt and pepper, to taste
2 large onions, sliced
4 carrots, diced
4 large potatoes, diced
8 cups beef stock
4 bay leaves
2 sprigs of rosemary
2 sprigs of thyme
½ cup red wine

### Directions
- Preheat the oven to 300°F.

- Place the canola oil in a large skillet and warm it over medium-high heat. Pat the short ribs dry and season generously with salt.

- Place the short ribs in the skillet and cook, while turning, until they are browned all over.

- Transfer the browned short ribs to a Dutch oven with the onions, carrots, potatoes, stock, and bay leaves. Cover, place the Dutch oven in the oven, and cook until the short ribs are fork-tender and the meat easily comes away from the bone, about 3 to 4 hours.

- Remove from the oven, strain through a fine sieve, and reserve the cooking liquid. Set the short ribs and vegetables aside.

- Place the reserved liquid in a pan with the rosemary, thyme, and red wine. Cook over high heat until the sauce has reduced and started to thicken. Season with salt and pepper. Divide the short ribs and vegetables between the serving plates and spoon 2 to 3 tablespoons of the sauce over each portion.

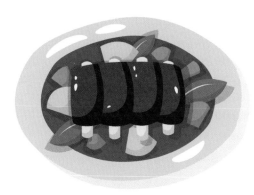

### 418

Get a seasonal job working as a shopping mall Santa Claus or Christmas elf.

### 419

Do you have a famous recipe that everyone in your family is always begging you to make? Why not make a few batches ahead of time and freeze them to give away as Christmas gifts? The gift of not having to cook dinner is priceless.

### 420

Make your own "stained glass" drawings with markers, crayons, and wax paper. Draw the outline of what you want to draw in marker, then color it in with crayons and hang it in the window for a colorful surprise.

### 421

Attend a hockey game.

### 422

If your kids are old enough to live on their own, gift each of them their own Christmas tree topper that matches the one you have on your family tree. You can turn this into a yearly tradition if you'd like.

### 423

Make a Popsicle stick picture frame ornament. Glue four Popsicle sticks together in the shape of a frame using hot glue. Cut a photograph down to the size of the square and glue the frame over it. Then, use a piece of yarn to hang on the tree. You can paint the Popsicle sticks or add glitter, if you want.

### 424

Make a holiday-themed bird feeder using an empty 2-liter bottle, two wooden spoons, and string. Drill two holes in the bottle big enough for the spoons to go through, making the holes slightly bigger on the end where the spoon head will be. Attach the string to the cap of the bottle, fill the bottle with birdseed, and place the spoons through the holes. The seeds should fall out onto the spoons.

### 425

Have a shelf cleaning day where you donate old books to your public library. This is a great way to free up shelf space for incoming new books.

### 426

Have a Christmas karaoke night.

### 427

Camp out in the snow.

### 428

Make holiday sun catchers. Buy festive colored gems from your local craft store. Take an unmatched container lid and arrange the gems on the lid, then cover up to the rim of the lid with clear glue. Allow to dry, then hang on the nearest window and enjoy.

### 429

Book one night in a fancy hotel nearby for a little staycation with the family.

# 430
# Make a classic Linzer tart.

## Ingredients

1 cup granulated sugar
12 tablespoons unsalted butter, at room temperature
1 teaspoon lemon zest
2 whole eggs
1¼ cups all-purpose flour
1 cup almond flour, toasted in the oven until golden
½ teaspoon cinnamon
¼ teaspoon cloves
1 tablespoon cocoa powder
¼ teaspoon salt
¾ cup raspberry jam, with or without seeds

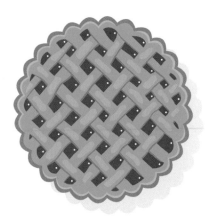

## Directions

- Cream the sugar, butter, and zest until smooth and creamy. Add the eggs one by one, scraping the bowl between each addition.

- Mix all the dry ingredients together. Add the dry ingredients to the butter mixture and mix in slowly. Be careful not to over-mix. Wrap the dough in 2 equal packages and chill until firm, about 1 hour.

- Preheat the oven to 350°F. On a lightly floured surface, roll out half of the dough and line a 9-inch tart pan with it. You can use your fingers to press any dough that cracks or breaks off back into the pan.

- Roll the second piece out to a 10-inch round and use a knife to cut strips ¾-inch wide.

- Fill the crust with the raspberry jam. Make a lattice top with the strips you cut. Bake for 35 to 40 minutes or until golden.

**431**

Make melted crayon artwork to decorate for the holidays by gluing crayons to a canvas and using a hair dryer to create cool patterns.

**432**

Nothing says holiday family time like great manners. Take an etiquette class as a family and then put your new manners to the test at a dinner party with friends.

**433**

Watch a Christmas movie while wrapping presents. Be sure to pick a classic movie that everyone has seen before, so you can concentrate on wrapping.

**434**

See a play at your local theater.

**435**

Make a Christmas wish tree. Use a mini countertop Christmas tree or a piece of paper cut out in the shape of a pine tree and hang it on the wall. Have each member of your family write down a wish that they have this Christmas and tape or hang them from the tree. Some good ideas might be, "100% on my next spelling test," or "A year of good health for the entire family."

**436**

Make marshmallow snowmen using toothpicks and small pieces of candy.

### 437
Create a family holiday cookbook with all your favorite Christmas recipes.

### 438
Create a Christmas snack tray to enjoy on movie night. Fill a tray with all those holiday treats you have laying around and set it out on the coffee table for everyone to enjoy. You can include things like fudge, nuts, holiday-themed snack mixes, cookies, and more.

### 439
Create your own indoor "slide-in" movie theater by bringing your family's sleds indoors and sitting on them to watch holiday movies.

### 440
Make vegan vanilla ice cream. Combine 2 (14 oz.) cans of coconut milk, ¾ cup maple syrup, seeds of 2 vanilla beans, and 1 teaspoon sea salt in a blender or food processor and blitz until combined. Refrigerate overnight. Pour the chilled mixture into an ice cream maker and churn until the desired consistency is achieved. Freeze for 1 hour before serving.

### 441
Attend a Christmas market.

### 442
See who can list the most names for Santa Claus without looking them up.

# 443
## Make a Vin Chaud cocktail.

### Ingredients
  1 (750 ml) bottle of inexpensive red wine
  1 star anise pod
  2 pieces of ginger (fresh or candied)
  3 cloves
  2 cardamom pods
  1 tablespoon orange zest
  1 tablespoon lemon zest
  ½ cup honey
  ½ cup Cognac
  Cinnamon sticks, for garnish

### Directions
- Place all the cocktail ingredients, except for the Cognac, in a saucepan and bring to a simmer. Remove from heat, add the Cognac, pour into mugs, and garnish with cinnamon sticks.

**Tip:** If you'd prefer something other than Cognac, pear eau-de-vie and Calvados are solid alternatives.

# 444

## Make a Gin Pom-Pom cocktail.

### Ingredients
  6 mints leaves
  1 part gin
  1 part pomegranate juice
  Juice of 1 lime wedge
  1 lime wheel, for garnish
  Pomegranate seeds, for garnish

### Directions
· Tear the mint leaves in half and place them in a cocktail shaker filled with ice. Add the gin, pomegranate juice, and lime juice and shake vigorously. Strain into a rocks glass filled with ice and garnish with the lime wheel and pomegranate seeds.

### 445

See if your town has a Polar Express event happening and take your kids to enjoy it.

### 446

Make thumbprint Christmas lights by covering your thumb in ink or paint and using the print to make the bulb of the lights. Be sure to hang them all over your house.

### 447

Make customized Christmas stockings using fabric paints.

### 448

Make gift giving last longer on Christmas morning by leaving clues to the hidden location of their gift.

### 449

Enjoy nature by going for a snowshoe hike. If you're lucky enough to live in a place that might get snow around Christmas time, this can be a fun way to get out of the house and enjoy the beauty of the snow. If you don't own your own snowshoes, you can always rent them or borrow them from a friend.

### 450

Make reindeer out of brown paper lunch bags by drawing faces on the bottom of the bags and adding antlers or using markers to add any colors you'd like.

### 451

Make a donation to your local library.

**452**
Spend the evening visiting with an older friend or relative who might be lonely near the holidays.

**453**
Watch holiday baking shows together and try out some of the recipes you see.

**454**
Go on a Christmas cruise.

**455**
Using air-dry clay or salt dough, have your kids make handprint ornaments for the tree. Be sure to write the date and their names on the ornaments so you can look back on them for years to come.

**456**
Host a holiday paint-and-sip event.

**457**
If you have a college student in your life, gift them with cooking utensils they may not have thought to buy for themselves, like a vegetable peeler or a colander.

**458**
Sew a family quilt. Have everyone in your family that knows how to sew put together their own squares and sew them together to make a family quilt.

**459**
Gift the booklover in your life a classic novel that they may not have read yet.

'Twas the night
when all through
a creature
not even

before Christmas,
the house, not
was stirring,
a mouse.

—Clement C. Moore

# 460
# Make chocolate and walnut fudge.

### Ingredients
- 1 cup chopped walnuts
- ¾ lb. quality bittersweet chocolate, chopped
- 2 oz. unsweetened baker's chocolate, chopped
- 1 stick of unsalted butter
- 2 cups granulated sugar
- 1 teaspoon pure vanilla extract

## Directions

- Preheat the oven to 350°F and line a square 8-inch cake pan with heavy-duty aluminum foil so that the foil extends over the sides. Spray the foil with nonstick cooking spray.

- Place the walnuts on a baking sheet, place it in the oven, and toast the walnuts for 5 to 7 minutes, until lightly browned. Remove from the oven and set the nuts aside.

- Place the chocolates and the butter in a heatproof mixing bowl and set aside. Place the sugar in a deep saucepan and cook over medium heat until it has dissolved and is boiling.

- Continue to cook, while stirring constantly, until the sugar reaches 236°F. Pour the sugar over the chocolates and butter in the mixing bowl. Whisk until smooth and then stir in the toasted walnuts and vanilla.

- Spread the fudge in an even layer in the cake pan. Refrigerate until the fudge is set, about 2 hours. Use the foil to lift the fudge out of the pan and then cut the fudge into squares.

### 461

Make a permanent white elephant number kit. Instead of having to write out numbers for everyone to choose from each year, find a decorative gift bag and paint rocks or wooden chips with each number. Be sure to use holiday-themed paints.

### 462

Make a Christmas fortune teller to find out if you're naughty or nice. You can also include Christmas dares if you want to spice things up.

### 463

Keep a book full of family quotes and wise sayings, then read through them around the holidays.

### 464

Watch *Bing Crosby's Merrie Olde Christmas* (1977).

### 465

Visit a model train exhibit.

### 466

Christmas is the perfect time to give homeless pets some extra love. Check with your local shelter to see if they accept help from volunteers or allow visitors. You can always donate blankets and food to the shelter if you don't have time to volunteer.

### 467

Go ice skating. Indoor or outdoor, this is a fun way to get out of the house and get some exercise.

**468**
Visit a living Nativity.

**469**
Decorate everyone's toothbrushes with a festive handle made out of pipe cleaners.

**470**
Go for a ski-do ride.

**471**
Use candy canes as Christmas tree decorations.

**472**
Make a Christmas movie calendar. Plan a different movie to watch each night in the weeks leading up to Christmas.

**473**
Treat everyone at your office to pizza or sandwiches for lunch.

**474**
Eat Christmas-colored candy corn.

**475**
Place a decorative garland and lights above your kitchen cabinets if you have the space.

**476**
Many farms put on special events around the holidays such as horse and buggy rides, hot apple cider, and even visits with Santa. Check out one of your local farms and take part in the festivities.

# 477
## Make Christmas ornament earrings.

**Tools**
Pliers
Fishhook ear wires (available at most craft stores in the jewelry section)
Miniature Christmas bulb ornaments

**Directions**
- Use pliers to twist open the loop on the end of one ear wire. Slide it through the fixture on one ornament. Use pliers to close. Repeat to make an identical pair.

# 478
## Make ice marbles.

### Tools
1 bag party balloons
Food coloring
Water

### Directions
- This activity requires temperatures below freezing. To make the ice marbles, drop a few drops of food coloring into the bottom of each balloon and fill the balloons up with water.

- Tie each ballon so there is as little air as possible trapped in the balloon, so the water fills as much of the balloon as possible. Once the balloon is tied, shake it well to mix the food coloring. Repeat with the remaining balloons.

- Leave outside overnight or until the water inside the balloons has frozen solid. Use scissors to cut the balloons open and peel the rubber away from the frozen water inside. These can be used as outdoor decorations.

### 479

Make stars out of glittery
pipe cleaners and string them
together for a festive garland.

### 480

Go Christmas caroling.
If this sounds outside your
comfort zone, consider getting
a group of kids and adults
together to visit a local senior
center or nursing home.
It's easier to get in the
spirit with a large group.

### 481

Take a trip to your local
art museum.

### 482

Gift an evening of free
childcare to a friend that
could use a night out.

### 483

Check with your child's
teacher to see if anyone in
your child's class may be
struggling near the holidays.
See if the teacher can
coordinate an anonymous
donation of clothes, toys, or
food that can go directly to
that child's family.

### 484

Start your own Christmas
blog to document your
holiday festivities.

### 485

Keep a dish of your favorite
holiday candy (like red and
green M&Ms or peppermints)
on the coffee table or counter
to enjoy throughout the
holiday season.

### 486

Host your own mini "baking show." Split everyone up into teams and give a baking challenge. If kitchen space is a problem, you can stagger the bakes so that each team is in the kitchen at a different time.

### 487

Hold an international holiday food sampling night.

### 488

Instead of a list of things you want your family and friends to buy for you, try making a list of things you want to give yourself this Christmas, like practicing self-care, or starting a new workout.

### 489

Make a tradition of reading "Twas the Night Before Christmas" as a family on Christmas Eve.

### 490

Make a hand wreath. Using a pencil, trace handprints onto sheets of red and green construction paper and cut out. Begin gluing hands together in the shape of a wreath so that the base of the palm forms the inner circle, and the fingers are pointing out. You can adjust the amount of hand cutouts to the size wreath you would like to make. Tie a bow with a piece of ribbon or yarn and attach to the top of the wreath for decoration.

# 491

## Make Rice Krispies treats.

### Ingredients

5 tablespoons unsalted butter
1 lb. large marshmallows
1 (16 oz.) bag of miniature marshmallows
½ teaspoon pure vanilla extract
½ teaspoon salt
8 cups crispy rice cereal
Red and green sprinkles (optional)

### Directions

· Place the butter in a large saucepan and warm over medium heat until melted. Add the large and miniature marshmallows and cook, while stirring frequently, until the marshmallows have melted.

· Add vanilla and salt and stir to incorporate. Add the cereal and stir gently until the cereal is evenly coated.

· Remove the saucepan from heat and pour the mixture into a greased 9 x 13-inch baking dish. Let the mixture cool.

· When the mixture is cool enough to handle, press it into an even layer. Top with the sprinkles, if using, and let stand for 30 minutes.

· Cut the mixture into bars and serve.

**Tip:** These can be cut into fun shapes using cookie cutters before they've hardened. Be sure to grease the cookie cutters with cooking spray to prevent them from getting stuck.

# 492
# Make a gluten-free raspberry almond tart.

## Ingredients
1 gluten-free pie crust
5 tablespoons unsalted butter, softened
½ cup granulated sugar, plus 1 tablespoon
Dash of salt
1 egg, plus 1 egg white
¾ cup almond flour
½ teaspoon almond extract
1½ cups fresh raspberries

## Directions
- Preheat the oven to 375°F. In a large bowl, cream butter with sugar until mixture is light and fluffy. Add salt.

- Stir in the egg and egg white until thoroughly combined, then the flour and almond extract. In a separate bowl, stir the raspberries with the extra tablespoon of sugar.

- Sprinkle about ⅓ of the berries on the crust. Top with the almond-and-egg mixture and add the remaining raspberries on top.

- Put the skillet in the oven and bake for about 40 to 45 minutes, until a knife inserted near the center comes out clean. Allow to cool completely before serving.

### 493
Have a Christmas card swap. Ask your guests to bring old Christmas cards from when they were kids, then place them all in a basket and distribute one card to each guest. Whoever matches the card with the right person first, wins.

### 494
Attend a Christmas event at a local winery. This makes for the perfect Christmas date night.

### 495
Set up a train under your Christmas tree. You can even use wrapped presents to create tunnels and bridges for your train.

### 496
Read *Miracle on 34th Street* by Valentine Davies.

### 497
Clear the snow from cars or sidewalks around your neighborhood.

### 498
Make boxes of assorted Christmas cookies to give out to your coworkers.

### 499
Instead of cutting down a Christmas tree or buying a fake one, check your local garden store for a live, potted Christmas tree. These trees can be planted outside after Christmas to continue growing.

**500**
Read *The Year of the Perfect Christmas Tree* by Gloria Houston.

**501**
Watch "The Andy Williams Christmas Show."

**502**
Practice random acts of kindness throughout the holidays.

**503**
Make Christmas wreath decorations out of bow tie pasta. First, paint the pasta green, sprinkle with glitter, and allow to dry. Then, glue onto paper to form a circle. Add a ribbon at the bottom and display.

**504**
Spend time with the family by hosting a board game tournament on Christmas Eve.

**505**
It's especially difficult for soldiers to be overseas during the holidays, so why not send them something to make the season a little brighter? Look for an organization that will pair you with a service member or send a care package to someone you know.

**506**
Take a class on soap-making and use what you learn to create homemade gifts for your friends and family.

# 507
## Make butter pecan bread pudding.

### Ingredients
½ cup chopped pecans
½ cup brown sugar
1 stick of unsalted butter
4 cups day-old bread pieces
2 cups heavy cream
1 teaspoon pure vanilla extract
½ cup granulated sugar
Caramel topping, warmed

## Directions

- Warm a cast-iron skillet over medium-high heat. When the skillet is hot, add the pecans and shake the skillet for 1 to 2 minutes as they toast. When the pecans are fragrant, transfer them to a bowl with the brown sugar and half of the butter. Toss to coat and set the mixture aside.

- Place the remaining butter in the skillet and warm over low heat. When it is melted, add the pieces of bread and shake the skillet until they are coated. Transfer the pieces of bread into a large baking dish.

- Place the heavy cream, vanilla, and granulated sugar in a mixing bowl and whisk until combined. Pour the mixture over the bread and shake the baking dish to evenly distribute. Cover the dish with aluminum foil and let stand in a cool place for 30 minutes.

- Preheat the oven to 350°F. Remove the foil, place the dish in the oven, and bake until the pudding is set and browned at the edges, about 45 minutes. Remove from the oven and let cool for 5 to 10 minutes before generously drizzling the caramel over the top.

One of the most
the world is the
the living room

glorious messes in

mess created in

on Christmas Day.

—Andy Rooney

**508**

Make winter travel a little easier by adding warm blankets to your car for long road trips. These are especially handy on cold mornings while your car is still heating up.

**509**

Have a good old-fashioned snowball fight. Just remember: no headshots.

**510**

Gift the wine enthusiast in your life a set of monogrammed wine glasses.

**511**

Schedule a professional family photo shoot for your next Christmas card.

**512**

Have a Christmas party where everyone brings a favorite food from their childhood as a contribution to the meal.

**513**

Visit a local antique shop or thrift store and look for fun, vintage Christmas decorations to add to your seasonal décor.

**514**

Go on a candy scavenger hunt at your favorite store and see who can find the most festive holiday items, like a peanut butter chocolate Santa Claus or reindeer poop candies.

**515**

Watch *Noel* (2004).

### 516

Make paper cup lanterns using plain paper cups, LED lights, and markers to decorate the exterior however you want. Be sure to leave some spaces blank to let enough light shine through.

### 517

If you live nearby, visit the Mummer's Day Parade in Philadelphia on January 1st.

### 518

Have you ever wanted to learn how to knit? How about making preserves? Try picking up a new skill this holiday season. This is a great way to spend the colder months and you might even be able to make homemade presents.

### 519

Go sledding together.

### 520

If you love decorating for Christmas but aren't sure where to place or hang all of your decorations, consider temporarily packing away your normal home décor. Clearing space away will make your Christmas decorations feel more purposeful and reduce the clutter the season can bring.

### 521

Visit your favorite department store the day after Christmas and pick up discounted decorations and wrapping paper for next year.

# 522
## Make Mexican hot chocolate.

### Ingredients

3 cups whole milk
1 cup half-and-half
3 cinnamon sticks
1 red chili pepper
¼ cup sweetened condensed milk
1½ lbs. semisweet chocolate chips
½ teaspoon pure vanilla extract
1 teaspoon grated nutmeg
½ teaspoon salt
Whipped cream, for garnish
Red pepper flakes, for garnish (optional)

### Directions

- Place the milk, half-and-half, cinnamon sticks, and chili pepper in a saucepan and cook over medium-low heat for 5 to 6 minutes, making sure the mixture does not come to a boil. Remove the cinnamon sticks and chili pepper.

- Add the sweetened condensed milk and whisk until combined. Add the chocolate chips and cook, while stirring occasionally, until the chocolate is melted. Add the vanilla, nutmeg, and salt and whisk until combined.

- Ladle into warmed mugs, top with whipped cream, and garnish with red pepper flakes, if desired.

# 523

## Make felt peppermint ornaments.

### Tools
White and red felt
Fabric glue
Gold thread

### Directions
- Begin by cutting the white felt into the shape of a circle. You can trace the rim of a glass if you are having trouble cutting the felt in the right shape. Cut two small triangles out of the white felt to use for the wrapper.

- Cut small, bar-like rectangles to use as the red stripes on the peppermint. Add a dot of glue to the tip of each white triangle and attach one on each side of white circle.

- Use a toothpick to spread fabric glue onto one of the red rectangles and glue it to the side of the circle that you did not attach the wrapper ends to. Continue gluing red stripes all around the edge of the circle to create a candy-stripe affect.

- On the back side of the circle, place a small dot of glue and attach the thread to hold up the ornament.

### 524

Have a soup and bread party. Invite all of your friends to bring a pot of soup or a loaf of bread to the party and spend the evening sampling each other's recipes.

### 525

Read *A Merry Little Christmas* by Mary Engelbreit.

### 526

Make a Christmas survival kit. This can include hot cocoa packets, extra tape, gift tags, ribbon, tinsel, and more.

### 527

Give a family member your secret recipe for a dish they love.

### 528

Make a miniature Christmas dinner out of oven bake clay and set it up in your window as a decoration.

### 529

Take a nature walk in the snow.

### 530

Make a donation to a local charity that provides heating oil for people in your area who are struggling to keep their homes warm.

### 531

Go to the store and have everyone pick out their favorite Christmas candle, then take turns lighting them.

**532**
Read the poem "Christmas Trees" by Robert Frost.

**533**
Give your local sanitation worker a thank you gift for all their hard work around the holidays.

**534**
Go see a Christmas pageant at a local church.

**535**
Watch *National Lampoon's Christmas Vacation* (1989).

**536**
Give everyone in your family a sweater to keep them warm through the winter months.

**537**
Sing Christmas carols around the fire.

**538**
Live somewhere without snow? Have a snowball fight with pom-poms.

**539**
Make a gingerbread house (see the recipe for gingerbread cookies on page 20).

**540**
When Christmas shopping, focus on things that your loved ones could really use, but wouldn't buy for themselves, like new dress shoes or a gift certificate for a car detailing.

# 541

## Serve cinnamon rolls on Christmas morning.

Ingredients

    All-purpose flour, for dusting
    1 (26.4 oz.) package of frozen biscuits
    2 teaspoons cinnamon
    ¾ cup dark brown sugar, firmly packed
    4 tablespoons unsalted butter, at room temperature
    1 cup confectioners' sugar
    3 tablespoons half-and-half
    ½ teaspoon pure vanilla extract

### Directions

- Preheat the oven to 375°F. On a flour-dusted work surface, spread the frozen biscuit dough out in rows of 4 biscuits each. Cover with a clean dishcloth and let sit for about 30 minutes until the dough is thawed but still cool.

- Combine the cinnamon and brown sugar in a small bowl. When the dough is ready, sprinkle flour over the top and fold it in half, then press it out to form a large rectangle (approximately 10 x 12-inches). Spread the butter over the dough, then top with the cinnamon-and-sugar mixture.

- Roll up the dough, starting with a long side. Cut into 1-inch slices and place them in a lightly greased cake pan.

- Place in the oven and bake for about 35 minutes, until the rolls are cooked through in the center. Remove from the oven and allow to cool slightly.

- Make the glaze by combining the confectioners' sugar, half-and-half, and vanilla in a small bowl. Drizzle over the warm rolls and serve.

**542**
Visit an aquarium
over the holidays.

**543**
Have a contest to see who
can find the ugliest Christmas
ornament to put on the tree.

**544**
Give hats and gloves as
Christmas gifts.

**545**
Can't find a toy drive in
your area? Start one yourself.
Check with local food pantries
or homeless shelters for advice
on how to distribute the toys
to families in need.

**546**
Play ice hockey.

**547**
Have your child make a
salt dough ornament (see page
254) for everyone in their class
with the name of their school
or teacher and the date.

**548**
Work on a Christmas
crossword puzzle together.

**549**
Watch *Alvin and the
Chipmunks: A Chipmunk
Christmas* (1981).

**550**
Create a funny
Christmas card by editing a
photo from a family vacation
you took this year so that each
of your family members is
wearing a Santa hat.

### 551
Visit an ice castle. There are plenty to choose from all around the world, just do some research to find one close to you. Some even offer overnight lodging.

### 552
Make delicious caramel popcorn. Place freshly popped popcorn in a large bowl and drizzle with warmed caramel, to taste. Toss until the popcorn is evenly coated. Pour the popcorn onto a parchment-lined baking sheet in an even layer. Let stand for 30 minutes before serving. If you can resist eating it all, package this popcorn in a decorative tin and give to coworkers and neighbors as a gift.

### 553
Decorate mason jars to use to hold Christmas presents, like hot cocoa mix or sea salt scrub (see page 228).

### 554
Grow a Christmas cactus. This festive holiday plant blooms around Christmas every year and can live for 20 to 30 years.

### 555
Hide chocolate coins around the house and see who can find the most over the holiday season.

### 556
Visit a holiday craft fair.

# 557
## Make pecan, chocolate, and bourbon tarts.

### Ingredients
**For the Dough**
- 1½ sticks of unsalted butter, at room temperature
- ⅔ cup cream cheese, at room temperature
- 1½ cups all-purpose flour
- ½ cup powdered sugar

**For the Filling**
- 2 tablespoons unsalted butter
- 1½ cups brown sugar
- 2 eggs
- 1½ cups chopped pecans
- ½ cup semisweet chocolate morsels
- 1 tablespoon bourbon
- 24 pecan halves, for topping

### Directions
- Cream the butter and cream cheese in a stand-mixer until just combined. Combine flour and powdered sugar in a bowl. Add the dry ingredients to the butter and cream cheese and mix until just combined. Finish working the dough with your hands.

- Spoon approximately 1 tablespoon of dough into each ungreased tart pan mold. Press and spread dough in the mold and allow to sit.

- To make the filling, heat the oven to 350°F. In a small bowl or saucepan, melt the butter and set aside.

- In a medium mixing bowl, mix the brown sugar and eggs with a spatula. Add the melted butter and mix well. Fold in the chopped pecans, then add the chocolate morsels and bourbon. Mix until all ingredients are combined.

- Fill tart dough molds with filling to just below the tops. Add pecan halves on top of each tart. Bake for 20 to 22 minutes or until the crust is a light golden brown. Let cool 15 minutes before removing from pan.

### 558
Find the funniest Christmas accessories you can and then take a family photo together.

### 559
Create colorful holiday salt paintings. All you need is card stock, glue, salt, and liquid watercolors. First, let your kids trace out a festive design on the card stock using glue. Next, cover the glue in salt and gently shake off the extra. Then, using the liquid watercolors and a paint brush, add color to the drawing. The paint will travel along the salt and make incredible pictures. Keep in mind this project may take up to two days to dry.

### 560
Read the poem "Good King Wenceslas" by John Mason Neale.

### 561
Hang some mistletoe above your door.

### 562
Make Christmas-themed beaded safety pins using holiday-colored micro beads and safety pins. You can wear these on your clothes or string them together for a safety pin chain.

### 563
Hang solar lanterns from tress outside your yard to brighten up the winter months.

### 564
Start a pocket change piggy bank to keep on your counter during the holidays. Everyone in the family can add their spare change throughout the season, and at the end of the holidays you can donate the funds to a local charity.

### 565
Attend a Christmas choir performance.

### 566
Play the card game spoons but swap out the spoons for candy canes.

### 567
Go to the movies on Christmas day.

### 568
If you live or work on a farm, think about dressing the barn up for Christmas by hanging up lights and decorations that are safe for the animals that live there.

### 569
Make miniature wreaths from mason jar rims by looping string tightly around the edge of the rim and adding holly berries, ribbon, or anything else you'd like.

### 570
Keep dessert simple by whipping up a loaf of fresh gingerbread using a boxed mix. Just be sure to serve with fresh whipped cream.

"Maybe Christmas,"
"doesn't come

Maybe Christmas...
a little

he thought,
from a store.
perhaps... means
bit more!"

—Dr. Seuss, *How the Grinch Stole Christmas!*

# 571
# Make chocolate and almond crinkle cookies.

## Ingredients
- ⅔ cup slivered almonds
- 2 tablespoons granulated sugar
- 6 oz. bittersweet chocolate, finely chopped
- ¼ cup whole milk
- 1 stick of unsalted butter
- 1½ cups packed light brown sugar
- 2 large eggs, at room temperature
- ½ teaspoon pure almond extract
- 2 tablespoons unsweetened cocoa powder
- 2 teaspoons baking powder
- ½ teaspoon salt
- 2¾ cups all-purpose flour
- ¾ cup confectioners' sugar

## Directions
- Preheat the oven to 350°F. Place the almonds on a baking sheet and toast for 5 to 7 minutes, until lightly browned. Remove from the oven and transfer to a food processor. Add the granulated sugar and pulse until the mixture is very fine.

- Combine the chocolate and milk in a microwave-safe bowl and microwave on medium for 15-second intervals until melted and smooth, removing to stir in between each interval.

- Combine the butter and brown sugar in a mixing bowl and beat at low speed with a handheld mixer to combine. Increase the speed to high and beat for 3 to 4 minutes, until light and fluffy. Add the eggs one at a time and beat until incorporated. Add the chocolate-and-milk mixture, almond extract, cocoa powder, baking powder, and salt and beat for 1 minute. Slowly add the flour and beat until a stiff dough forms. Stir in the almonds and place the dough in the refrigerator for at least 2 hours, until it is firm.

- Preheat the oven to 350°F and line two baking sheets with parchment paper. Sift the confectioners' sugar onto a sheet of waxed paper. Remove tablespoon-sized portions of the dough, form them into balls, and roll each ball in the confectioners' sugar until well coated. Place the balls 2 inches apart on the baking sheets, place in the oven, and bake for 14 to 16 minutes, until the cookies are cracking, and the edges feel dry. Remove, let cool for 2 minutes, and then transfer to wire racks to cool completely.

### 572
Find out if any organizations in your area are running a food drive and donate.

### 573
Make snow cones.
If you live somewhere with snow, you can just collect fresh snow outside, or you can invest in a snow cone maker. You can cut back on the amount of sugar by using sugar-free juice instead of traditional syrups or use festive flavors like chocolate or cinnamon.

### 574
Try and reenact your favorite Christmas movie from memory. If you're feeling brave, you can record your attempts to watch back later.

### 575
Read *The Jolly Christmas Postman* by Janet Alhberg.

### 576
Offer to run errands for a family member.

### 577
Make jewelry out of recycled objects and give them as gifts.

### 578
Make cookie mix jars to give as gifts. Combine dry ingredients from your favorite cookie or brownie recipe in a large glass jar. Try adding the ingredients to the jar in layers for an eye-catching effect and be sure to include baking instructions.

## 579

Make a Christmas pinata using papier-mâché and a balloon, just be sure to leave an opening to add candy. You can use festive colors to paint the outside or decorate it to look like a Christmas tree.

## 580

Do you know anyone who got married this year or bought their first home? Give them a small box filled with a few nice ornaments to hang on their first Christmas tree.

## 581

If you have young children, help them make a handprint picture to give to their parent or grandparents as a gift.

## 582

Play the penguin waddle game. Separate into teams of three or more. Set up a racecourse and have each team member place an inflated balloon between their knees. The goal is to waddle from one end to the other and back without dropping the balloon and hand it off to their teammate. If the balloon is dropped, that racer has to start over. Whichever team finishes first, wins.

## 583

Whether festive holiday nail polish is your style or not, a trip to the salon to get a manicure or pedicure together can be a great way to unwind from the stress of the holidays.

# 584
## Play the gift wrap game.

### Tools
- 1 main present
- Lots of gift wrap
- Tape
- Small gifts like candy, toys, or plastic rings

### How to play:
- Wrap the main present with as many layers of wrapping paper as you want.

- Once the present has been wrapped, have each player go in a circle and unwrap one layer of wrapping paper. Then, they pass it to the next person. Play music in the background while people unwrap the gift and pause it randomly.

- Whoever is holding the gift when the song is paused gets a smaller gift, and the person to unwrap the final layer of wrapping paper gets the main present.

# 585
## Make Danish rugbrød.

### Ingredients
5½ cups dark rye flour
1¼ cups rye chops, soaked in water overnight, boiled for 15 minutes, and drained
2 cups rye sourdough starter
1⅔ cups lukewarm water
1 cup dark beer
2 tablespoons molasses
1½ teaspoons salt

### Directions
- Combine all ingredients but the salt and let rest for 15 minutes, covered. Add the salt and combine well.

- Place in two small (8 x 4 x 2½-inch) loaf pans and put them in two food-approved plastic bags.

- Let rest at room temperature until the dough has nearly doubled, about 4 hours.

- Preheat the oven to 320°F and bake for about 2½ hours. Let cool for a whole day before slicing.

**586**

Read *A Porcupine in a Pine Tree: A Canadian 12 Days of Christmas* by Helaine Becker.

**587**

Is your family camera shy? Instead of sending out a Christmas card with the entire family on it, make one of just the family pets.

**588**

Organize a winter beach cleanup as a way to give back during the holidays.

**589**

Send Christmas goodies through the mail to people who can't make it home for the holidays.

**590**

Build an Advent goal box together and take out one goal every day of December. This can include things like "spend more time as a family" or "do something nice for our neighbors."

**591**

Do a Christmas themed puzzle. Set it up on a table that's out of the way and set a goal of finishing it by Christmas Day. Then, frame the finished puzzle and display each Christmas.

**592**

Sit down together as a family and make a list of all the things you value and wish for each other in the coming year.

### 593
If you live somewhere with snow, leave "Santa footprints" in the snow outside. You can also use two skis to make "sleigh tracks" in the backyard.

### 594
Have a breakfast buffet on Christmas morning. Instead of cooking one big meal to share on Christmas morning, have a variety of make-ahead options available, like yogurt, Danishes, and plenty of hot cocoa. This will help cut down the craziness of Christmas morning.

### 595
Leave gifts at your neighbor's doorstep and hide to watch their response.

### 596
Listen to *Ultimate Christmas* by Frank Sinatra.

### 597
Make packages filled with Christmas cookies to deliver to your neighbors.

### 598
Make honey-roasted figs. In a medium nonstick sauté pan, add 2 tablespoons honey and warm over medium heat. Halve 4 Black Mission figs and place them face down in the pan. Cook for 5 minutes, or until golden brown. Sprinkle ⅛ teaspoon cinnamon over the figs and gently stir to coat. Remove figs from the pan, top with crumbled goat cheese, and serve.

# 599
# Make cookies and candy bark.

### Ingredients
12 oz. semisweet chocolate, broken into pieces
12 oz. white chocolate, broken into pieces
1 (8 oz.) bag mini York Peppermint Patties
½ cup Oreo cookie pieces, crushed
½ cup Andes Thin Mints, broken into small pieces
½ cup crushed peppermint candy
2 teaspoons vegetable oil (no substitutions)

### Directions
- Line a cookie or baking sheet with parchment paper. In separate strong plastic bags, use a hammer or meat pounder to break the cookies and candies into pieces or shards. Put the pieces in separate bowls and set aside.

- Melt the semisweet chocolate in a double boiler, or in a bowl or saucepan set over simmering water. Alternately, put the chocolate pieces in a microwave-safe bowl and melt in 20- to 30-second increments, stirring after each one, until the chocolate is just melted. You want to melt the chocolate slowly.

- Once melted, stir in 1 teaspoon of vegetable oil. Pour the chocolate onto the cookie sheet and use a spatula to spread it as evenly as possible over the parchment paper. Press mini peppermint patties into this bottom layer, but don't overdo it. Leave room for the additional cookies and candy that will go on the next layer. Refrigerate for about 15 minutes, until set.

- Next, melt the white chocolate the same way, being careful to melt it slowly and thoroughly. Add 1 teaspoon of vegetable oil once melted and incorporate thoroughly. Pour the white chocolate over the set semi-sweet chocolate, using a spatula to spread it as evenly as possible. Sprinkle the cookie and thin mint pieces liberally and evenly over the white chocolate, pressing lightly into the layer of white chocolate.

- Finish by sprinkling shards of peppermint candy on top. Refrigerate for about 30 minutes, until set. Lift the candy off the parchment paper, breaking into pieces as you do. Refrigerate the bark until ready to eat.

### 600

Learn to say "Merry Christmas" in another language. Here are some to get you started:

**French:** *Joyeux noël!*
(zhwa-yeu noh-ehl)
**Spanish:** *¡Feliz Navidad!*
(feh-lees nah-bee-dahd)
**German:** *Fröhliche Weihnachten!*
(froh-leash-eh vine-ach-ten)

### 601

Make Christmas-themed décor by gathering twigs from your yard and spray painting them with silver and gold spray paint. You can arrange them in vases to make a tasteful, modern addition to your seasonal decorations. The best part about these decorations is you can leave them up all winter.

### 602

Pair off into teams. Each person should draw their teammate as their favorite character from a Christmas movie, TV show, or book. Hang all of these pictures up for everyone to view when they're done.

### 603

Volunteer to help out at a local Christmas parade this year. These types of events often require a lot more coordination than meets the eye, and they wouldn't be able to happen without the help of volunteers.

### 604

Play Christmas freeze dance using your favorite holiday music.

### 605

Make peppermint-scented playdough. In a pot, combine 1 cup salt, 1 tablespoon cream of tartar, and 2 cups flour. Add 2 cups water, 1 tablespoon vegetable oil, and 1 tablespoon peppermint extract and stir together over medium heat for 3 to 5 minutes, until the dough forms a ball. Remove from heat and allow to cool. Once cool, knead the dough until it is smooth. Add red food coloring and more peppermint extract, if desired, and knead until combined. Store in an airtight container or plastic bag when not in use.

### 606

Join a holiday fun run.

### 607

Make a family music video by lip syncing to your favorite Christmas songs.

### 608

Pair off into teams of two. Tie one person's right hand to their teammate's left hand. Each team's goal is to wrap a gift together using their free hands. Whoever wraps their present the best within a 1- to 3-minute time limit, wins.

### 609

Have a family slumber party in the living room on Christmas Eve.

### 610

Donate warm blankets to your local homeless shelter.

# 611
## Make gluten-free chocolate peppermint biscotti.

### Ingredients
- 1 cup brown rice flour
- ½ cup unsweetened cocoa powder
- ⅓ cup potato starch
- 3 tablespoons tapioca starch
- 1 teaspoon xanthan gum
- ½ teaspoon gluten-free baking powder
- ¼ teaspoon salt
- 1 stick of unsalted butter
- 2½ cups confectioners' sugar
- 2 large eggs
- ½ teaspoon peppermint extract
- 1 (3 oz.) package cream cheese, softened
- ¾ cup peppermint bark, broken into pea-sized pieces

## Directions

- Preheat oven to 350°F. Line a baking sheet with parchment paper.

- Combine the rice flour, cocoa, potato starch, tapioca starch, xanthan gum, baking powder, and salt in a medium bowl. Whisk to combine thoroughly. Set aside.

- In a large bowl, combine butter and 1¼ cups confectioners' sugar. Beat at medium speed with an electric mixer until combined, then increase to high speed and beat for another 3 to 4 minutes, until light and fluffy. Add the eggs and peppermint extract and beat for another minute to combine.

- Slowly add the dry ingredients to the butter mixture and beat until a stiff dough forms. Transfer the dough to the cookie sheet and form into a rectangle about 12 x 3-inches. Bake for about 40 minutes, until golden. Remove from oven and allow to cool on cookie sheet about 30 minutes.

- On a cutting board, transfer the cookie and cut into slices on the diagonal using a sharp, serrated knife. Arrange pieces cut-side down on the baking sheet and bake for an additional 15 minutes. Transfer cookies to a wire rack to cool completely.

Reflect upon your

of which every

not your past

which all men

present blessings—
man has many—
misfortunes, of
have some.

—Charles Dickens, *A Christmas Carol*

### 612

Ask a family member
to teach you a skill of theirs
that you admire. You can even
work together to make gifts
for the season.

### 613

Make a Grinch wreath.
Cover a burlap wreath with
craft moss and, using a hot
glue gun, glue securely into
place. Add two paper eyes near
the center of the wreath and
top with a Santa hat.

### 614

Have a wacky meal
this holiday season by letting
each family member pick out
one dish to make. It's okay if
the choices don't necessarily
go together, like pancakes
and meatloaf.

### 615

Do you have a friend
or family member who is
saving for something big?
You can get them started in
saving up for it by decorating
a jar or piggy bank in the
theme of what they are saving
for. Then, add a small donation
to the jar and give it as
a Christmas gift.

### 616

Make a family calendar
together for the new year.
You can include things like
birthdays, family holidays, or
even your favorite memories,
like the one-year anniversary
of when you adopted
your family pet.

### 617

Do a Christmas needlepoint.

### 618
Bring a fruitcake to your holiday Yankee Swap.

### 619
Make button snowflake ornaments. Use three Popsicle sticks to make a snowflake shape. Using a hot glue gun, glue them together at the center. Glue buttons to the "arms" of the snowflake in whatever pattern you desire. Allow to dry. Then, glue a loop of yarn onto the back of the snowflake and display.
Tip: You can use colorful Popsicle sticks to add even more festive flare.

### 620
Design holiday PJs for your kids' favorite stuffed animals or toys.

### 621
Listen to *Choirs and Carols: An NPR Christmas* on npr.org.

### 622
Put a Christmas wreath on your mailbox post.

### 623
Make paper straw snowflakes by overlapping patterned paper straws to make the snowflake "arms." Glue a circular piece of paper into the center to hold the straws together and add a large button or piece of holly for added flare.

### 624
Read the poem "The Three Kings" by Henry Wadsworth Longfellow.

# 625
## Make caramel and pecan bars.

### Ingredients
 ½ lb. pecan halves
 1 cup all-purpose flour
 ⅓ cup confectioners' sugar
 ¼ teaspoon salt
 2 sticks of unsalted butter
 1 large egg, at room temperature
 ½ teaspoon pure vanilla extract
 ¼ teaspoon pure almond extract
 Whole milk, as needed
 ¾ cup packed light brown sugar
 ¼ cup light corn syrup
 ¼ cup heavy cream

### Directions
- Preheat the oven to 375°F. Line a square 8-inch cake pan with aluminum foil and grease the foil with nonstick cooking spray.

- Place the pecans on a baking sheet, place them in the oven, and toast until lightly browned, about 5 minutes. Remove and set aside.

- Place the flour, confectioners' sugar, and salt in a food processor and blitz for 5 seconds. Add half of the butter and pulse until the mixture resembles a coarse meal.

- Place the egg, vanilla extract, and almond extract in a small cup and whisk until well combined. Drizzle the liquid into the food processor and pulse until a stiff dough forms. If dough is too dry, add milk in 1-teaspoon increments until it holds together.

- Transfer the dough to the prepared baking pan and press down on it until it is firmly packed and approximately ¾-inch high. Place the dough in the freezer for 15 minutes. Remove, prick with a fork, place in the oven, and bake until lightly browned, about 10 minutes. Remove and let cool.

- While the crust is baking, place the remaining butter, brown sugar, and corn syrup in a saucepan and bring to a boil over high heat, while whisking constantly. Boil for 2 minutes, remove pan from heat, and stir in the heavy cream and toasted pecans, being careful as the mixture will splatter.

- Spoon the butter-and-pecan topping over the baked crust and smooth the top with a rubber spatula. Place in the oven and bake until the topping is bubbling and dark brown, about 20 minutes. Remove from the oven and let cool completely in the pan before cutting into bars.

## 626
Catch snowflakes
on your tongue.

## 627
Make corn flour Christmas
decorations. In a large box,
combine 1 part PVA glue
with 1 part corn flour until
they reach a dough-like
consistency. Flatten the dough,
then cut into shapes using
cookie cutters. Make sure to
make a small hole at the top
to hang them later. Place the
shapes on a baking tray and
allow to dry overnight. String
the ornaments and hang on
the tree or give as gifts.
Tip: These can be painted,
if desired, or left white.

## 628
Visit a Christmas village.

## 629
If you have a shed or garage,
decorate the inside with lights,
garlands, and even fake snow.

## 630
If you didn't cook the
holiday meal, offer to help
with the dishes.

## 631
Make a Christmas collage
with pictures cut out
of magazines.

## 632
Learn holiday-themed jokes
and have a comedy hour.

## 633
Create your own Winter
Olympics, complete with
tinfoil medals, of course.

**634**

Play Christmas I Spy
with your kids on a drive
around your neighborhood.
If they're lucky, they might
even spot Santa himself.

**635**

Watch *The Santa
Clause* (1994).

**636**

Have everyone write a
funny poem about Christmas
and read them aloud.

**637**

Host a Christmas book club.
Choose any Christmas-themed
title and get a group of friends
to all read the same book.
Then, gather one evening
for book discussion and
some holiday treats.

**638**

Host a themed potluck.
You can include themes like
"casseroles" or "classic
holiday favorites."

**639**

Have a Christmas
trivia tournament. Divide
into teams and assign a quiz
master to ask the questions.
Each team gets one point for
every question they answer
correctly. After each team has
answered 50 questions, the
team with the most points
wins. You can find plenty of
Christmas trivia online or
make up your own questions.

**640**

Gift an adult coloring
book to a friend who
needs to de-stress.

# 641
## Play Christmas who am I?

### Tools
Markers
Index cards
Large rubber bands or headbands
Timer

### How to play:
- Write out as many animals, objects, and people you can think of, keeping to one per each index card. Make sure to shuffle them.

- Give each player a rubber band or headband. Each player draws an index card without looking at it and puts it on their headband.

- Start the timer for 30 seconds. Each player can ask as many yes or no questions about their index card as they can ask in 30 seconds, and the remaining players have to answer truthfully. If they guess what their card is, they can draw another index card and guess that one as well. Once the timer runs out, switch to the next person.

- At the end of three to five rounds, whoever has the most correctly guessed cards wins.

Santa Claus

# 642
## Make classic shortbread wedges.

### Ingredients
1 cup all-purpose flour, plus more for dusting
¼ teaspoon salt
¼ cup granulated sugar
1 stick of unsalted butter, chilled
½ teaspoon vanilla extract

### Directions
- Preheat the oven to 300°F. Place a 12-inch cast-iron skillet in the oven while making the dough.

- In a large bowl, combine the flour, salt, and sugar, and whisk to combine.

- Cut the butter into slices and add to the flour mixture. The best way to work it into the flour is with your hands. As it starts to come together, add the vanilla extract. Work the mixture until it resembles a coarse meal.

- Gather the dough into a ball. On a lightly floured surface, roll it out into a circle that's just smaller than the surface of the skillet. Slice the round into 8 wedges.

- Remove the skillet from the oven and place the wedges in it to recreate the circle of dough. Bake for about 45 minutes or until the shortbread is a pale golden color. Remove the skillet from the oven and allow to cool for about 10 minutes before transferring the cookies to a plate.

### 643

Pick a game like
ping-pong, air hockey,
or paper football and hold a
competition with all of your
family members.

### 644

If you have extra storage
space in your home, help a
friend out by offering to store
any large Christmas gifts they
are trying to hide in your
attic or garage.

### 645

Add food coloring and
water to spray bottles and
paint pictures in the snow
outside. This is a great activity
to do with kids, just remember
that a little food coloring
goes a long way.

### 646

Learn about how
people in other countries
celebrate Christmas.

### 647

Make a peppermint
wreath. Starting at the
inside edge of a foam wreath,
use a hot glue gun to glue
unwrapped peppermint
candies to the wreath, leaning
them in one direction, until
you have gone around the
whole wreath. Once you have
finished the first row, move to
the next section and alternate
the direction of the candies.
Repeat this until you have
covered the entire wreath with
candies. Once finished, loop a
ribbon around the wreath and
hang on your front door.

### 648
Put Christmas window decals on the windows in your home.

### 649
Have a red-and-green-themed meal.

### 650
Make handmade Christmas cards this year. Get out a variety of craft supplies and let everyone get creative.

### 651
Get everyone in your family matching winter hats.

### 652
Watch *Somewhere in Dreamland* (1936).

### 653
Make a Christmas scrapbook to keep on display during the holiday season. Be sure to leave extra space to add more memories each Christmas.

### 654
Serve a traditional British plum pudding with custard on Christmas. You can find the pudding and custard in specialty shops or order them online.

### 655
Play homemade holiday Jeopardy! You can print out your own questions or write them on index cards, and have each player make a buzzing noise before they answer a question.

# 656
# Make a Christmas kaleidoscope.

Tools
   Paper towel roll
   Scissors
   Aluminum foil
   White card stock
   Clear tape
   Plastic berry container
   Hot glue gun
   Red, green, and gold plastic beads
   Corrugated scrapbook paper

## Directions

- Measure the paper towel roll and cut a piece of aluminum foil and white card stock to be 1½ inches shorter than the length of the roll. Tape the aluminum foil to the card stock, keeping the foil as flat as possible. This will be your mirror. Cut the aluminum foil and card stock to the width of the inside of the roll by measuring the diameter of the roll, dividing in half, and then multiplying by three. Score the aluminum foil in three even lines, then fold into a triangle and tape, keeping the aluminum foil side facing inward.

- Trace the end of your paper towel roll and cut three circles from the plastic container at this size. Place one of the circles on the end of the roll and hot glue it into place. Insert the mirror triangle into the roll so it rests on the plastic surface. Turn over your tube and insert the second circle of plastic inside the tube so it rests on the end of the mirror and glue it in place.

- Add the colorful beads so they rest on the interior piece of plastic. Secure the last piece of plastic on the remaining open end of the roll.

- To make the spinner, take the corrugated scrapbook paper and cut so it is ½ the length of the roll. Then, wrap around the roll and secure the long edges using tape so the tube of paper can spin around the paper towel tube.

- If desired, cut a circle out of the remaining white card stock with a small hole in the center for the eyepiece. Tape onto the end of the tube that is farthest from the beads to finish the kaleidoscope.

### 657

Make hot fudge sundaes. Place as much hot fudge as you desire in the bottom of four tulip sundae dishes or bowls. Scoop vanilla ice cream into the bowls, then add more hot fudge. Top each sundae with whipped cream, pecans or walnuts, if desired, and a maraschino cherry.

### 658

Go on a Christmas sound scavenger hunt. Make a list of sounds you might hear during the holidays, like jingle bells, caroling, etc. and see who can identify the most sounds first.

### 659

Play pin the nose on the reindeer.

### 660

Set up an outdoor Nativity set.

### 661

Use tissue paper to create "stained glass" windows with festive shapes. Simply cut the tissue paper into fun shapes and then tape to the window with double-sided tape. If you are sure the tissue paper won't run, you can adhere them to your windows using a mix of soap and water and a paint brush.

### 662

Choose a charitable organization that is close to your heart and make a donation in an amount that fits your budget.

### 663

Make a winter bird feeder. Begin by tying 12 inches of string or yarn around 1 large pinecone so the cone can securely hang from the string. Using a butter knife, spread peanut butter over the pinecone in an even layer. Take a handful of birdseed and sprinkle it over the pinecone so that is sticks to the peanut butter. Repeat until the pinecone is completely covered in birdseed and no peanut butter is left exposed. Once finished, hang from a tree branch.

### 664

Make your own elf village outside using recycled materials, complete with doors, roads, and painted rocks.

### 665

The Christmas season can be exhausting, and you might not have the energy to cook an elaborate meal on Christmas day. Gift yourself with a day away from the kitchen by preparing your food ahead of time and stocking the fridge with snacks like veggie trays, cold cuts, and cheese plates.

### 666

Make candy sleds. Attach 2 candy canes to the bottom of a full graham cracker using frosting. Allow to dry. Form licorice into a horseshoe shape and attach to the front of the graham cracker using frosting. Decorate the sled with additional frosting and sprinkles.

At Christmas
good cheer,
comes but

play and make
for Christmas
once a year.

—Thomas Tusser

# 667
## Make borax crystal snowflakes.

**Tools**

3 (5-inch) pipe cleaners, plus 6 (1½-inch) pipe cleaners
Pencil
String
Mason jar
3 tablespoons borax
Blue food coloring (optional)
1 cup boiling water

**Directions**

- Twist the three 5-inch pieces of pipe cleaner together to form a snowflake shape with six points. Then, add the smaller pipe cleaners to the end of each point and bend into a triangle shape to complete the snowflake frame.

- Tie the snowflake to the pencil using a piece of string, leaving enough slack so that the snowflake does not touch the bottom of the jar, but can be covered with liquid.

- Combine the borax, 1 drop of food coloring, if using, and the boiling water. Pour the mixture into the jar and allow to sit overnight. Remove, dry, and display.

# 668
# Play reindeer games.

## Tools
Fake reindeer antlers
Red noses (optional, but recommended)
Plastic or paper rings

## How to play:
- The object of this game is to get as many rings on the reindeer's antlers as possible before time runs out. One player wears the antlers and nose, while their teammate tries to toss the rings onto the antlers.

- Mark a spot at least 5 feet away and have the antler-wearing player take their spot. The reindeer can try and help catch the rings, but they should not move any closer to the player and cannot use their hands. The team with the most rings on their reindeer wins!

### 669
Donate a Christmas wreath or tree to your child's classroom.

### 670
Make your own caramel corn. Place 12 cups freshly popped popcorn in a large bowl and drizzle warmed caramel over the top, to taste. Toss until the popcorn is evenly coated. Pour the popcorn onto a parchment-lined baking sheet in an even layer. Let stand for 30 minutes before serving.

### 671
Attach a bell to your pet's collar. They will spread Christmas cheer wherever they go!

### 672
Bring some Christmas joy to those who have to work on Christmas. Let them know you are grateful for what they do by bringing them a box of cookies or other Christmas goodies. This is an excellent way to thank the people who take care of you and your loved ones every day.

### 673
Make your own mailboxes and write letters to each other with your Christmas lists using specific addresses like, "Mom, in the study" or, "Tommy, on the front porch."

### 674
Build the ultimate snow fort together.

### 675

Leave "Santa footprints" near the fireplace using baking soda and a pair of boots. Just be prepared for some extra vacuuming later.

### 676

Make a point to sit down and chat with each of your family members one-on-one.

### 677

Make Mrs. Claus's apple cider. Combine 1 oz. spiced rum, ½ oz. apple schnapps, ½ oz. cinnamon schnapps, and a splash of lemon-lime soda in a cocktail shaker filled with crushed ice and shake until chilled. Strain into a shot glass and garnish with mint leaves, if desired.

### 678

Sure, it's nice to keep in touch with family and friends via social media at this time of year, but try to limit your family's screen time by having everyone put away their phones during family activities. After all, reconnecting people face-to-face is the reason for the season.

### 679

Take a nutcracker with you on all your Christmas adventures and take pictures of the nutcracker doing activities alongside your family. At the end of the holidays, make a scrapbook full of the nutcracker's photos.

# 680

## Make your own rock candy.

**Tools**
 4 mason jars
 Cotton thread
 4 pencils

**Ingredients**
 2 cups water
 4 cups granulated sugar
 2 drops of food coloring of choice (for a holiday theme, use red or green)

## Directions

- To begin, clean 4 glass mason jars with warm water. Cut 4 lengths of thread a few inches higher than each jar and tape each thread to a pencil. Wind the thread around the pencil until the thread dangles 1 inch from the bottom of the jar.

- Wet each thread with water and roll in granulated sugar. Set aside to dry.

- Add the water to a medium saucepan and bring to a boil. Add the sugar one cup at a time, stirring between each addition. Continue to stir, while boiling, until all of the sugar has been added and has completely dissolved. Remove the pan from heat.

- If using the food coloring, add to the mixture and stir until the syrup has a nice, even color. Allow to cool for 10 minutes.

- Pour the syrup into each jar. Then, lower the string into the jars and set the pencil across the top.

- Place the jars in a dark, quiet place and cover with plastic wrap or paper towels. The crystals should begin to form after 2 to 4 hours. If nothing has taken hold after 24 hours, you may need to repeat the recipe again.

- Once the rock candy has reached the desired size, remove, allow to dry, and serve.

### 681

Use some of your Christmas vacation time to visit a historical location you have never been to before.

### 682

Make a dyed flower bouquet. Begin by filling 2 vases each about halfway with water and stirring about five drops of red and green food coloring into each vase. Cut off the ends of white flowers, like daisies or carnations, and divide them between the red and green vases. Leave overnight. Once the flowers have achieved the desired amount of pigmentation, remove, discard the colored water solution, and put the flowers together in a large vase with plain water.

### 683

Gift the first book in a series that you love to a friend or family member.

### 684

Watch *Little Women* (2019).

### 685

Read *Annie and the Wild Animals* by Jan Brett.

### 686

Instead of spring cleaning, try Christmas cleaning to get rid of all that extra stuff you don't need. Just be sure to donate what you don't end up keeping.

### 687

Host a cookie swap with family and friends.

### 688
Listen to the yearly Christmas Eve broadcast of the Choir of King's College on bbc.co.uk.

### 689
If you know that a family member or friend will be away during the holidays, offer to look after their pets or plants to help relieve the stress of having to find someone to do it.

### 690
Each time it snows in December, use a ruler to record how many inches fell. Figure out the total amount of snow you got by Christmas time and compare to next year's snowfall.

### 691
Pull a wholesome Christmas prank by wrapping your coworker's workstation in wrapping paper. Don't go too overboard or your office might be next.

### 692
Make a family Christmas banner. Let each family member add to it using whatever craft materials they want. Make sure everyone signs their masterpiece.

### 693
Gift yourself an early Christmas present and sign up for a cooking class around October or November. Then, use your newfound skills during the holidays.

# 694
## Bake apple cider donuts.

### Ingredients
- 1½ cups apple cider
- 2½ cups granulated sugar
- 5 tablespoons unsalted butter, at room temperature
- 2 large eggs, at room temperature
- 3½ cups all-purpose flour, plus more for dusting
- 1¼ teaspoons salt
- 2 teaspoons baking powder
- 1 teaspoon baking soda
- 3½ tablespoons ground cinnamon
- ½ teaspoon grated nutmeg
- ½ cup buttermilk
- 1 tablespoon pure vanilla extract
- Canola oil, for frying

### Directions
- Place the apple cider in a saucepan and bring to a simmer over medium-high heat. Cook until the cider has reduced to approximately ⅓ cup. Remove from heat and let cool completely.

- Place 1 cup of the sugar and the butter in the mixing bowl of a stand mixer and beat until the mixture is pale and fluffy. Add the eggs one at a time and beat until completely incorporated before adding the next one.

- Place the flour, salt, baking powder, baking soda, ½ teaspoon of the cinnamon, and nutmeg in another mixing bowl, whisk to combine, and set the mixture aside.

- Add the buttermilk, the cooled reduced cider, and vanilla into the bowl of the stand mixer. Add the flour mixture and beat on low speed until combined.

- Generously dust a work surface with flour and place the dough on it. Pat it into a rectangle that is ¾ inch thick. Sprinkle the dough generously with flour, transfer to a parchment-lined baking sheet, cover with plastic wrap, and place in the freezer for 20 minutes.

- Remove the dough from the freezer and use a floured biscuit cutter or mason jar to cut it into rounds. Place the donuts on another parchment-lined baking sheet and place them in the freezer for 5 minutes.

- Place the remaining sugar and cinnamon in a bowl, stir to combine, and set the mixture aside.

- Add canola oil to a Dutch oven until it is 3 inches deep and heat it to 350°F. Working in batches of three donuts, place the donuts in the hot oil and fry until golden brown, about 1 minute. Turn the donuts over and fry for another minute. Transfer the cooked donuts to a paper towel-lined plate to drain.

- When the donuts are still warm but cool enough to handle, dredge them in the cinnamon-and-sugar mixture and serve immediately.

### 695

Make a winter cheese board. Finely chop ½ cup roasted nuts, herbs, and/or fruits as desired into a consistent blend. Roll or press a chilled 4 oz. log of fresh goat cheese into the blend. Allow to come to room temperature before arranging on a board with candied nuts, chocolate truffles, and fresh fruit.

### 696

Play Santa limbo by having each guest put on a Santa hat and a "Santa belly" made from a pillow under their shirt. Then, have everyone line up and try and limbo under a stick. Whoever can go the lowest wins.

### 697

Make a sea salt scrub to give as a gift. Combine 1 cup coarse sea salt and ½ cup coconut oil or olive oil in a large bowl and mix with a fork until the oil is fully incorporated into the salt. Add 4 to 5 drops of essential oil of choice and mix in. Store in an airtight container until ready to use.

### 698

Have a holiday masquerade party at your house, complete with masks and dancing.

### 699

Use a globe or map to randomly pick a continent or country, then learn about the winter holiday celebrations in that location.

### 700

Play twenty questions.
Make sure to stay on
the holiday theme.

### 701

Make chunky crayons as
a unique gift for a child in your
life. First, collect an assortment
of crayon nubs and remove
any paper. Preheat the oven to
275°F. Spray a muffin tin with
cooking spray and fill each
hole with crayon bits. If the
crayon pieces you have are too
large to fit in the tray, break or
chop them into smaller pieces.
Once you fill the tray, place it
in the oven and allow crayons
to melt for 5 to 7 minutes.
Remove tray from oven and
let cool completely before
removing from the mold.

### 702

Instead of letting opened
cards accumulate in a stack
on the counter, why not hang
them up where they can add to
your holiday décor? Try taping
them around a doorframe or
hanging them from a piece of
string with clothespins.

### 703

Read *The Snowy Day*
by Ezra Jack Keats.

### 704

Instead of gifting your
family members traditional
presents, give them a little
extra cash to go toward paying
off their student loans or
covering their rent. Sometimes
that added bit of help makes
all the difference.

# 705

## Make pom-poms for decorating presents.

**Tools**
    Rectangular piece of carboard
    Scissors
    Yarn (bulky preferred)

## Directions

- Take the carboard and cut a section, starting at the bottom middle, that is about ½ inch wide and goes ¾ of the way up the cardboard. You should have a shape that looks similar to a pair of high-waisted pants.

- Wrap the yarn around both "legs" of the cardboard in one continuous motion. Do not weave through the legs. Once you have a large amount of yarn wrapped around the legs, cut the end of the yarn.

- Using a second piece of yarn, tie a knot around the wrapped yarn, using the top space and bottom edge of the carboard you cut to thread the second piece of yarn through.

- Tie off the wrapped yarn as tightly as possible and remove from the carboard. It should look a little like a bow tie.

- Tie the yarn again in the same direction, pulling tighter as you go. Repeat this step two or three times.

- Using the scissors, cut the yarn where it loops around the edges. Fan out the cut yarn to finish the pom-pom.

To cherish peace
to be plenteous in
the real spirit

*and goodwill, mercy, is to have of Christmas.*

—Former President Calvin Coolidge

### 706
Watch *Frozen* (2013).

### 707
Divide your guests into teams of two to three players. Give each team a list with the alphabet on it. The goal of the game is to write down one holiday-related thing for each letter of the alphabet. Whoever answers the fastest with accurate answers, wins.

### 708
Visit Washington, D.C. and see the nation's capital dressed up for the holidays.

### 709
Start a book drive in your town to donate books to a local homeless shelter.

### 710
Use dried citrus slices (see page 79) to make a holiday garland. Thread an upholstery needle or book binder's needle with one yard of thin twine or waxed linen thread, leaving a two-inch tail. Make a loop at the long end of the thread and close with a sturdy knot. Begin threading the needle through the center of the fruit slices. Thread cranberries or wooden beads between each slice. This will allow light to shine through the fruit slices. When you get about six inches from the end of the thread, remove the needle and tie a loop in the end of the string. Hang the garland by the loops near a source of light.

**711**

Make a "nice list" of all the people who made your year better. Make sure to let them know that they made your list and why.

**712**

Make your own festive tongue twisters. Here are a couple to get you started "I see Santa's sleigh," Sally Slate says slyly. Through free Christmas trees three freezing breezes freely flew.

**713**

Learn about what other holidays take place during the winter months, and how different cultures celebrate community during the cold months of the year.

**714**

Go cross-country skiing on a local trail.

**715**

Nothing says Christmas like bundling up around a campfire. Have a bonfire in your backyard.

**716**

Make hot buttered rum. Muddle 1 tablespoon butter, 1 teaspoon brown sugar, dash of cinnamon, dash of nutmeg, and dash of orange zest in the bottom of an Irish coffee glass. Once ingredients are thoroughly mixed, add splash of vanilla extract, 6 oz. hot water, 2 oz. dark rum, and dash of allspice. Stir to combine and garnish with the cinnamon stick.

# 717
## Bake a king cake.

### Ingredients
⅓ cup whole milk
1¾ teaspoons active dry yeast
3 cups all-purpose flour, plus more for dusting
⅓ cup confectioners' sugar
¼ teaspoon grated nutmeg
1 teaspoon lemon zest
2 eggs
Yolk of 1 egg
1 teaspoon orange blossom water
6 tablespoons unsalted butter, cut into small pieces
1 teaspoon salt
5 tablespoons warm water (110°F)
3 tablespoons granulated sugar
Yellow, purple, and green food coloring (optional)
Candied fruit, roughly chopped

### Directions
- Place the milk in a saucepan and heat to 100°F. Add the yeast, gently stir, and let the mixture rest for 5 minutes.

- Place the mixture in a large mixing bowl. Add the flour, the confectioners' sugar, nutmeg, lemon zest, one of the eggs, the egg yolk, and the orange blossom water and beat until combined.

- Transfer the dough to the mixing bowl of a stand mixer fitted with the dough hook attachment. Work the dough and gradually incorporate the butter. When all of the butter has been incorporated, add the salt and work the mixture until it is very smooth. This should take about 20 minutes. Place the dough in a naturally warm spot and let it rise until it has doubled in size, about 1 to 1½ hours.

- Transfer the dough to a flour-dusted work surface and shape it into a ball. Place the ball in a 9 x 13-inch baking dish lined with parchment and flatten it slightly. Make a small hole in the center of the dough and use your hands to gradually enlarge the hole and create a crown. Cover and let stand for 1 hour.

- Preheat the oven to 320°F. Place the remaining egg and 1 tablespoon of the warm water in a measuring cup and beat to combine. Brush the crown with the egg wash. Place in the oven and bake until the crown is golden brown and a toothpick inserted into the center comes out clean, about 30 minutes.

- Place the sugar and the remaining warm water in a mixing bowl and stir until the sugar has dissolved. Add the food coloring, if desired, and stir to combine. Brush the hot crown with the glaze and decorate with the chopped candied fruit.

### 718

Leave a completed loyalty punch card at the register of your local coffee shop or café to be used by the next person in line.

### 719

Gift a family member an oil change for their car.

### 720

Visit Cape Cod for New England Christmas charm, shopping, and holiday-themed events. Be sure to ride the train to Christmas Town.

### 721

Keep a holiday journal and read it every Christmas to remind you of all the things you have to be grateful for.

### 722

Use sandcastle buckets and beach toys in the snow to build beautiful snow castles.

### 723

Invite your close friends or family members to a holiday PJ party.

### 724

Pick a small "Charlie Brown tree" as your Christmas tree instead of a traditional full one. Sometimes a small, spindly tree can be just as heartwarming as a more conventional one.

### 725

Have a Secret Santa gift exchange with your friends or coworkers.

**726**
Attend a tree lighting ceremony.

**727**
Make a chocolate truffle tart. In a small saucepan over medium heat, bring 1½ cups heavy cream to a boil. Add 12 oz. chopped bittersweet chocolate to a mixing bowl, and once the cream boils pour it over the chocolate and stir until it is smooth and no lumps show up on the back of your spatula or spoon. Stir in ¼ cup cubed unsalted butter and, if desired, 2 tablespoons liqueur of choice. Strain into the cooled tart shell and spread evenly. Do not touch the top or you will ruin your glossy finish. Refrigerate for a couple hours until set.

**728**
Make snow angels.

**729**
Allow everyone to choose one gift from under the tree to unwrap on Christmas Eve.

**730**
Go paper plate skating on linoleum by standing on paper plates and "skating" around the area. You can also try getting a running start and see how far you can "skate."

**731**
Have a kindness morning where each family member leaves sticky notes with positive messages on each other's doors for a nice wakeup surprise.

# 732
## Make holiday cookie pops.

### Ingredients
- 1 stick of unsalted butter, at room temperature
- ⅓ cup granulated sugar
- ⅓ cup packed dark brown sugar
- ½ teaspoon salt
- ½ teaspoon pure vanilla extract
- 1 cup all-purpose flour
- 1 cup miniature semisweet chocolate chips
- Lollipop sticks
- ½ lb. white, milk, or dark chocolate, melted
- Chopped nuts (optional)
- Red, green, or gold sprinkles (optional)

### Directions

- Place the butter, sugar, and brown sugar in the bowl of a stand mixer and beat until it is light and fluffy. Add the salt and vanilla and beat until combined.

- Add the flour in two batches and beat until almost all of it has been incorporated. Before the flour is completely blended in, add the chocolate chips and mix until well combined. Cover the dough with plastic wrap and place in the refrigerator for 1 hour.

- Line a baking sheet with parchment paper. Remove the mixture from the refrigerator and scoop out teaspoon-sized balls of dough. Roll into spheres and place on the baking sheet. Insert lollipop sticks into each sphere.

- Dip each pop into the melted chocolate until completely coated. Decorate them with nuts or sprinkles, if desired, and place them back on the baking sheet. Place in the refrigerator and chill until the chocolate is set, about 2 hours.

### 733

Make peppermint Marshmallow Fluff. Combine 2 cups Marshmallow Fluff, ¼ teaspoons peppermint extract, and 2 tablespoons crushed peppermint in an airtight container and mix well with a greased spatula. Cover until ready to use. Serve on ice cream, sandwiched between cookies, or in mugs of hot chocolate.

### 734

If you can't have your own fire, make your livingroom a little cozier this Christmas by playing recorded Yule log videos on your computer or TV. You can even find one paired with Christmas music or with sleeping pets on screen.

### 735

Hang sleigh bells on your Christmas tree.

### 736

Take an empty picture frame with you to your favorite winter location and use it in a holiday photo shoot. You can even paint the edge of the frame with festive colors to match the season.

### 737

Purchase good quality office supplies like sticky notes and nice pens and use them as stocking stuffers for the adults in your life.

### 738

Read *How the Grinch Stole Christmas!* by Dr. Seuss.

### 739

Teach your kids how
to play a group sport outside
on Christmas day. If there
isn't too much snow, consider
something like kickball
or basketball.

### 740

If you have a friend
from another country that
celebrates Christmas, ask
them what their favorite
Christmas tradition is and
see if you can celebrate
it together.

### 741

Grab your camera and go on
an outdoor photo hunt. Make
the objects you're looking for
line up with the holidays for a
fun Christmas activity.

### 742

Not able to go ice skating?
Go sock skating through
your house. Just be careful
around sharp corners.

### 743

Make collage ornaments.
Assemble a pile of various
paper scraps. Paint a thin layer
of Mod Podge onto a large
glass or plastic bulb ornament
and stick a piece of paper to it,
using your finger to gently rub
it down so it sticks. Continue
this process until the entire
ornament is covered to your
liking, applying extra Mod
Podge when needed. Hang
to dry before using.

### 744

Leave carrots outside for
Santa's reindeer.

# 745

# Make a pom-pom "snowball" catapult with your kids.

## Tools
   2 small Popsicle sticks
   2 large tongue depressors
   4 rubber bands
   Small, white pom-poms, to launch

## Directions
- Lay down a small Popsicle stick. Place 1 tongue depressor in the center of the small Popsicle stick, allowing about 1½ inches of the larger stick to rest over one side.

- Lay the second smaller Popsicle stick on top and rubber band both ends tightly so the tongue depressor is pressed between the two smaller ones.

- Place the second tongue depressor on top of the first one and rubber band the two short ends together about ½ inch from the tip. Using the last rubber band, crisscross the center of the two tongue depressors so the rubber band wraps around the base of the catapult and the top.

- To use your catapult, place a small object on top of the long end of the larger stick. Press down on the front short end of the stick and the longer end at the same time. Release the longer end and allow the small object to soar.

# 746
## Make muddy buddies.

### Ingredients
- 1 cup semisweet chocolate chips
- ¾ cup creamy peanut butter
- 1 teaspoon pure vanilla extract
- 9 cups square rice cereal
- 1½ cups confectioners' sugar

### Directions
- Place the chocolate chips and peanut butter in a microwave-safe bowl and microwave for 30 seconds. Remove from the microwave, add the vanilla, and stir until the mixture is smooth.

- Place the rice cereal in a large bowl and pour the chocolate-peanut butter mixture over the cereal. Carefully mix until the pieces are coated.

- Place the cereal into a large plastic bag and add confectioners' sugar. Seal the bag and shake until each piece is coated with sugar.

- Line a baking sheet with parchment paper and pour the cereal onto the baking sheet. Place the sheet in the refrigerator and chill for 30 to 45 minutes.

**747**

Make personalized ornaments for friends and family members.

**748**

When Christmas shopping this year, focus on giving gifts that can turn into fun activities for the long winter months ahead, like board games, sleds, ice skates, art supplies, and more.

**749**

Leave enough money on a vending machine to pay for the next person's snack.

**750**

Read *Rudolph the Red-Nosed Reindeer* by Barbara Shook Hazen.

**751**

Serve a traditional iced Christmas cake from the UK. These rich fruit cakes last longer than normal cakes and can be ordered online.

**752**

Make a candy garland for your tree. Thread a long piece of thick thread (about 1 to 2 yards) through a large upholstery needle, leaving a two-inch tail, and make a sturdy knot at the long end of the thread. Thread pieces of wrapped candy onto the thread by running the needle through the wrapper only. Continue until the garland reaches the desired length. Unthread the needle and tie off the garland, cutting off any extra thread before hanging up.

### 753

Have a Christmas tea party. There are plenty of delicious holiday themed teas available. Pair them with some freshly baked scones and a few tea sandwiches and you'll be ready to take on an afternoon of wrapping gifts.

### 754

Find a holiday concert. Christmas is the perfect time to hear an orchestra or local musician play live.

### 755

Decorate a wreath with pinecones and holly. You can use red, white, silver, and gold spray paint on the pinecones to make them even more festive.

### 756

Send specialty nuts for a sugar-free gift option.

### 757

Make a Shirley Temple. Pour 1 tablespoon grenadine into the bottom of a glass, then add 1 cup ginger ale and stir until fully incorporated. Garnish with the maraschino cherries.

### 758

Make a Christmapolitan cocktail. Combine 1½ oz. vodka, 1 oz. St-Germain, 1 oz. cranberry sauce, ½ oz. lime juice, 2 dashes of fig bitters, and dash of Tabasco in a cocktail shaker filled with ice and shake vigorously. Strain into coupe and tie a red ribbon around the stem.

It's Christmas
night of the year
a little nicer,
easier, we cheer

Eve! It's the one when we all act we smile a little a little more.

—*Scrooged* (1988)

# 759

## Make honey nut truffles.

### Ingredients

- ½ cup peanut butter
- ¼ cup honey
- ¼ teaspoon salt
- 1 cup quality semisweet chocolate chips

### Directions

- Place the peanut butter, honey, and salt in a bowl and stir until well combined. Place teaspoon-sized balls of the mixture on a parchment-lined baking sheet and then place in the refrigerator for 1 hour.

- Remove the baking sheet from the refrigerator. Place the chocolate chips in microwave-safe bowl. Microwave on medium until melted, removing to stir every 20 seconds.

- Dip the balls into the melted chocolate until completely covered. Place them back on the baking sheet. When all the truffles have been coated, place them in the refrigerator and chill until the chocolate is set.

# 760
## Make a classic pumpkin pie.

### Ingredients
1 (14 oz.) can of pumpkin puree (not pumpkin pie filling)
1 (12 oz.) can of evaporated milk
2 eggs, lightly beaten
½ cup granulated sugar
½ teaspoon salt
1 teaspoon cinnamon
¼ teaspoon ground ginger
¼ teaspoon ground nutmeg
1 pre-baked pie crust

### Directions
- Preheat the oven to 400°F.
  In a large bowl, combine the
  pumpkin puree, evaporated milk,
  eggs, sugar, salt, cinnamon, ginger,
  and nutmeg. Stir to combine thoroughly.

- Working with the crust in the pie plate, fill it with the pumpkin mixture.
  Smooth the surface with a rubber spatula.

- Put the pie in the oven and bake for 15 minutes. Reduce the heat
  to 325°F and bake for an additional 30 to 45 minutes, until the
  filling is firm and a toothpick inserted in the middle comes
  out clean. Remove the pie from the oven and allow to cool
  before serving.

### 761

Have a hands-free marshmallow eating contest. Whoever can get the most marshmallows into their mouth without using their hands wins.

### 762

Wrap everyone's bedroom doors in wrapping paper on Christmas Eve.

### 763

Use a Santa hat as a cute tree topper instead of an angel or a star.

### 764

Pass along a family heirloom as a Christmas gift to one of your children or grandchildren.

### 765

Save herbs from your garden in the summer and hang them in bushels to dry for the winter. Dried, homegrown herbs make a nice gift at Christmas.

### 766

Make stove-top popcorn. Heat 1 tablespoon vegetable oil in a thick-bottomed pot over medium heat. Drop one kernel in the pot as the oil is heating; when it pops, pour in ½ cup of kernels and ½ teaspoon salt, stirring to coat in oil. Partially cover the pot with the lid and allow the popcorn to pop. When most of the kernels have popped, remove from heat and pour into a bowl. Season with additional salt or butter, if desired.

## 767

Make a conscious effort not to stress over the details and just enjoy Christmas as it happens.

## 768

Encourage your whole family to read through the holidays by making a reading chart where every family member keeps track of what books they have read. You can even make it a contest to see who can read the most books by Christmas Eve.

## 769

Go to the movies as a family. There are usually plenty of big blockbusters playing around the holidays, so make sure to take advantage of your vacation time and check one out.

## 770

Visit a holiday light show.

## 771

Catch up with an old friend by making time to go Christmas shopping together. You will have the chance to catch up and have fun together, while also checking important things off of your Christmas to-do list.

## 772

Make soap snow. Place 1 unwrapped Ivory soap bar on a microwave-safe plate, put in the microwave, and heat on high for 1 to 2 minutes, until the soap has stopped expanding and a soap cloud is left behind. Keep in mind this only works with Ivory soap!

# 773
## Make salt dough ornaments.

### Ingredients
  2 cups flour
  1 cup salt
  1 cup water
  Paint and glitter of choice
  String

### Directions
· Preheat oven to 200°F. Combine flour and salt
  in a large mixing bowl. Gradually add water 1
  tablespoon at a time, mixing as you go.

· Once all the water is incorporated, turn the dough out onto a well-
  floured work surface and knead for about 10 minutes, adding more flour
  or water as needed.

· Once the dough reaches your desired consistency, roll out and cut out
  the dough. Use a toothpick to make a hole at the top of each "cookie"
  and place on a baking sheet.

· Bake for 1 to 2 hours, or until the dough has fully hardened. Remove
  from oven and let cool completely.

· Decorate the ornaments with paint and glitter, then thread string
  through the holes to hang on the tree.

# 774
## Add this vegan rice pudding to your dessert menu.

### Ingredients
- 3 (14 oz.) cans of coconut milk
- 1 cup arborio rice
- ½ cup granulated sugar
- 3 strips of orange zest
- 1 teaspoon cinnamon
- ½ teaspoon grated nutmeg
- Pod of 1 vanilla bean
- ½ teaspoon salt

### Directions
- Place all of the ingredients in a saucepan and bring to a gentle boil over medium-low heat. Reduce heat to low and simmer, while stirring occasionally, until the rice is tender and the mixture is thick, about 25 minutes.

- Remove from heat and remove the orange zest and the vanilla pod. Let stand for 5 minutes. Serve warm or place in the refrigerator to chill for 5 minutes.

### 775

Blow bubbles in really cold temperatures to see them freeze.

### 776

Have a Christmas cookie secret Santa. Put everyone's names into a hat and have everyone draw a name. Instead of a traditional gift, each person makes their secret Santa a batch of cookies. Try to guess who your gifter is based on what kind of cookies they make.

### 777

Make a story book advent calendar. Wrap one picture book for each night leading up to Christmas and have your child unwrap one to read every night.

### 778

Have donuts for breakfast Christmas morning.

### 779

Make stained glass cookies (see page 16) into ornaments for your tree by making small holes in the top of each cookie with a toothpick before baking. Once the cookies have cooled completely, lay them out on baking sheets and leave in a dry place at room temperature for one week. After the cookies have dried out, spray them with crafter's shellac or hairspray to preserve. Thread decorative string through the holes and hang them on the tree out of reach of pets or small children. When storing or gifting these ornaments, be sure to label them as inedible.

### 780

Make chocolate-covered popcorn. Place 1½ lbs. semisweet chocolate chips in a microwave-safe bowl. Melt in the microwave on medium, removing to stir every 20 seconds. Once melted, remove from the microwave and stir until smooth. Divide 2 bags of popcorn between two bowls, season each one with salt and nutmeg, to taste, and toss to combine. Drizzle the melted chocolate over the popcorn and toss to coat. Line a baking sheet with parchment paper and pour the popcorn onto the baking sheet. Refrigerate for 30 minutes before serving.

### 781

Read *A Christmas Carol* by Charles Dickens.

### 782

Mix things up and give your family pet a smooch under the mistletoe.

### 783

Read *The Nutcracker and the Mouse King* by E. T. A. Hoffmann.

### 784

Learn to say "thank you" in another language. Here are some to get you started:
**French:** *Merci* (mer-sea)
**Spanish:** *Gracias* (gra-sea-as)
**German:** *Danke* (dan-ke) or the more formal *dankeschön* (dan-ke shern)

### 785

Spend the afternoon coloring with family.

# 786
# Make homemade nougat.

## Ingredients
Whites of 3 large eggs
3 cups granulated sugar
⅓ cup light corn syrup
1 cup honey
1 cup water
Zest of 1 lemon
Seeds of 2 vanilla beans
¾ teaspoon sea salt
1 cup slivered almonds, toasted

## Directions
· Place the egg whites in the mixing bowl of a stand mixer and beat until frothy. Set aside.

· Place the sugar, corn syrup, honey, and water in a saucepan and bring to a boil over medium-high heat. Cook until the mixture is 300°F.

· With the mixture running on low, add a splash of the hot syrup to the egg whites. When the eggs have been tempered, pour the rest of the hot syrup into the mixture and gradually increase the speed until the mixture is light and frothy. Add the lemon zest, vanilla seeds, salt, and slivered almonds and continue to run the mixer until the mixture has cooled considerably, about 15 to 20 minutes.

· Pour the mixture onto a greased, rimmed baking sheet and let cool completely before slicing into bars, about 1 hour.

# 787
# Make fruit- and nut-filled chocolate candies.

## Ingredients
½ lb. bittersweet or dark chocolate, chopped
1 tablespoon fleur de sel
2 tablespoons chopped dried cherries (optional)
2 tablespoons chopped roasted almonds (optional)
2 tablespoons chopped pistachios (optional)

## Directions
- Place the chocolate in a microwave-safe bowl. Melt in the microwave on medium, removing to stir every 20 seconds. When melted, remove from the microwave and stir until smooth.

- Scoop teaspoons of the melted chocolate into your chosen mold or onto a parchment-lined baking sheet. Sprinkle the fleur de sel on top and then place the dried cherries, roasted almonds, and/or pistachios on the chocolates, if desired. Transfer to the refrigerator and chill until set, about 30 minutes.

### 788

Enjoy homemade eggnog. In a bowl, beat 6 eggs until frothy. Whisk into the eggs ½ teaspoon vanilla extract, ¼ teaspoon grated nutmeg, 1 cup granulated sugar, ¾ cup brandy, ⅓ cup dark rum, 2 cups heavy cream, and 2 cups milk. When thoroughly combined, refrigerate until ready to serve.

### 789

Make your own personalized license plates, then attach them to your stockings to use as name tags.

### 790

Visit a candy store around the holidays.

### 791

For a unique gift, get someone a magazine subscription on a topic that interests them.

### 792

Make a Christmas snack-mix. In a large bowl, mix together red and green M&Ms, peanuts, dried cranberries, marshmallows, small pretzels, white chocolate chips, and popcorn and enjoy. Tip: Package the mix into individual jar-sized servings to use as gifts. You can even decorate the jars with curled ribbon.

### 793

If your whole family can't be together on Christmas, organize a family video call with your loved ones.

**794**
Build an ice skating rink
in the backyard.

**795**
Tour a candy factory
near you and see how all
the candy is made.

**796**
Make a snow globe in a jar.
Pour water into a glass jar
with a lid until it is full, then
add 1 tablespoon of glitter. Use
superglue to attach a figurine
of choice to the inside cover of
the jar. It should be attached so
that when the jar is closed and
sitting upside down with the
lid on the counter, the figurine
stands right-side up. Allow the
glue to dry fully before placing
the lid on the jar. Shake and
watch the glitter settle.

**797**
Serve virgin mimosas on
Christmas morning. Pour 3 oz.
orange juice into a champagne
flute, top with 3 oz. Sprite or
ginger ale, and garnish
with an orange slice.

**798**
Be sure to include
your pets in the holiday
festivities. A long walk with
your dog after your Christmas
meal or some sleepy cuddles
with your cat while you watch
a Christmas movie will make
sure your pet feels included
in all the holiday fun.

**799**
Have a completely
candlelit dinner together. The
only electric lights allowed are
your Christmas lights.

# 800
## Make a Christmas crayon rubbing.

### Tools
   2 sheets of regular copy paper
   Ballpoint pen
   Crayon in color of choice with paper removed
   (preferably red or green)

### Directions
- Begin by placing the two pieces of
  paper one on top of the other. Use the
  ballpoint pen to draw a simple picture
  (try a snowflake or a Christmas stocking).
  Press down firmly enough with the pen
  so the drawing makes an impression on
  the piece of paper underneath. Remove
  the top piece of paper.

- Lay the crayon flat on top of the bottom piece of paper and gently
  rub the crayon over the impression. The crayon will not color in the
  indentation and a picture will emerge.

# 801
## Make chai-poached pears.

### Ingredients
3 bags of chai tea
2 cinnamon sticks
4 whole cloves
2 teaspoons grated nutmeg
½ cup granulated sugar
4 ripe pears, left whole or peeled and sliced

### Directions
- Bring a saucepan of water to a boil. Add the tea bags, cinnamon sticks, cloves, and nutmeg, reduce the heat, and simmer for 10 minutes. Turn off the heat and let mixture steep for 30 minutes.

- Remove spices and tea bags from the water. Add the sugar and cook over low heat, while stirring, until the sugar is dissolved. Place the pears in the simmering tea and cook, while spooning the tea over the pears, until they are fork-tender, about 40 minutes. Turn the pears in the water as they cook to ensure that they are cooked evenly.

- Remove the pears from liquid, transfer them to the serving dishes, and spoon some of the liquid over the top.

Christmas is a

of rejoicing but

season not only
of reflection.

—Winston Churchill

### 802
Watch *Frozen II* (2019).

### 803
Make molasses snow candy. In a medium saucepan, mix 2 parts molasses with 1 part brown sugar and bring to a boil. Reduce heat to medium and cook for 5 to 6 minutes. Pour the contents of the pan into a cup with a spout and pour over the snow, forming small shapes like circles or squiggles. The snow will harden the molasses mixture into a candy-like substance. Store in an airtight container or eat right away.

### 804
Randomly pay for someone else's photos with Santa.

### 805
Make a clothespin Nativity using clothespins, markers, scraps of fabric, and glue.

### 806
Read *The Tailor of Gloucester* by Beatrix Potter.

### 807
Visit Disney World or Disney Land around Christmas to see one of the most extravagant Christmas displays in the country.

### 808
Who doesn't like the Muppets? Try to sing "The Twelve Days of Christmas" while each person does their best impression of a Muppet.

### 809
Play a Christmas memory game. Lay out a bunch of different holiday-themed items and cover them with a blanket. Each player is given a piece of paper and writing utensil. Give each player 60 seconds to look at the pile of objects without writing anything down. Then, cover the objects back up and have them write down as many things as they can remember. Whoever remembers the most objects, wins.

### 810
Cut down a real Christmas tree. Nothing beats the whole family heading out into the snow to pick out a tree together. It also makes for a great photo opportunity.

### 811
Instead of setting out candy for Christmas, set out bowls of fresh fruit for a healthy, refreshing treat.

### 812
Set aside the time to have quality, in-person conversations with the people you love.

### 813
If you're in the mood for some calming background music, listen to *Songs for Christmas* by Sufjan Stevens.

### 814
Paint rocks with holiday decorations and leave them around your neighborhood as a surprise.

# 815
## Make cheesecake-filled strawberries.

### Ingredients

⅓ cup heavy cream

1 (8 oz.) package of cream cheese, at room temperature

½ cup confectioners' sugar

1 teaspoon pure vanilla extract

¼ teaspoon salt

2 pints of fresh strawberries, hulled and cored

4 graham crackers, ground, for topping (optional)

Slivered almonds, for topping (optional)

### Directions

- Place the heavy cream in a mixing bowl and beat it until soft peaks form. Add the cream cheese, confectioners' sugar, vanilla, and salt and beat until the mixture is light and fluffy. Transfer the mixture into a piping bag or a large, resealable plastic bag.

- Pipe the mixture into the cavities in the strawberries until it is mounded on top. If using a plastic bag to pipe the mixture into the strawberries, cut a small opening in one of the bottom corners and squeeze the mixture into the cavity you made in the strawberries. You want the filling to form a mound on top of the strawberries without overflowing.

- Sprinkle graham cracker crumbs or slivered almonds on top and then place the stuffed strawberries in the refrigerator for 1 hour before serving.

## 816
Gift someone a nice set of cocktail glasses for Christmas.

## 817
Have a "no stuff" Christmas where instead of giving each other physical items, you gift your family and friends an experience or an act of service, such as being on dish duty for the entire week, taking a family member to a special restaurant, or a voucher for a free haircut or car wash.

## 818
See if anywhere around you is having a Christmas boat (or sled) brigade and join in.

## 819
Did you take a vacation with family or friends this year? Make a scrapbook with pictures from the trip to give as a Christmas gift.

## 820
Make peppermint white hot chocolate. In a saucepan over medium heat, combine 2 cups whole milk and 4 oz. white chocolate, broken into pieces, and heat slowly, stirring until the chocolate is just melting. Stir in ¼ teaspoon peppermint extract and continue to heat until thoroughly melted and combined. Use a whisk to beat the hot chocolate for a minute or two to make it light and foamy. Pour into mugs and top with whipped cream and white peppermint bark pieces.

### 821
Hang Christmas lights in areas of the house you wouldn't ordinarily think of, like your bedroom or even the bathroom.

### 822
Gift someone a monthly bus pass.

### 823
Go to a trampoline park together.

### 824
If your child has a special doll or stuffed animal that they are very attached to, surprise them by putting out a tiny stocking for their toy. Make sure to personalize it with the toy's name.

### 825
Make dried fruit potpourri. In a large pot, combine 6 dried fruit slices (see page 79), 6 cloves of star anise, 5 cinnamon sticks, 2 teaspoons ground nutmeg, 1 teaspoon salt, 1 tablespoon cloves, and 2 bay leaves with 5 cups water. Bring to a slow boil over medium-high heat, reduce heat, and then simmer to diffuse the scent. Remove pot from heat when done with the scent.

### 826
Make holiday stress balls using rice, red and green balloons, and a funnel. Simply funnel the rice into an uninflated balloon and tie it off at the end for an easy stress reducer.

# 827

## Make honey-roasted turnips with hazelnuts.

### Ingredients

16 small turnips, trimmed and quartered
¼ cup olive oil
½ cup honey
Salt and pepper, to taste
½ cup hazelnuts, toasted and chopped
¾ cup crème fraîche
¼ cup thinly sliced chives
Zest and juice of 1 lemon

### Directions

· Preheat the oven to 350°F. Place a 12-inch cast-iron skillet over medium-high heat for 5 minutes.

· Place the turnips, olive oil, and honey in a large bowl, season with salt and pepper, and toss to coat. Place the turnips in the skillet, cut side-down, and transfer the skillet to the oven. Roast until tender, about 30 minutes.

· To serve, sprinkle the hazelnuts over the turnips, drizzle the crème fraîche, and top with chives and lemon zest and juice.

# 828
## Make white chocolate bark.

### Ingredients
1 lb. white chocolate, chopped
½ cup dried cherries or cranberries
½ cup chopped pistachios

### Directions
- Place the chocolate in a microwave-safe bowl. Melt in the microwave on medium, removing to stir every 20 seconds. When melted, remove from the microwave and stir until smooth.

- Line a baking sheet with parchment paper. Pour the melted chocolate onto the baking sheet and spread it into an even layer, making sure not to spread it too thin.

- Sprinkle the cherries or cranberries and pistachios onto the chocolate and lightly press down to ensure that they stick. Place in the refrigerator until set, about 30 minutes.

- When the chocolate is set, break the bark into large pieces and serve.

### 829

Hold a candy cane hunt. Like an Easter hunt, hide candy canes all around your home or backyard. Send kids (or adults) on the hunt for these tasty treats equipped with a stocking to store their loot.

### 830

Who says barbeques are just for summer? Clear the snow off the grill and cook up something special for Christmas dinner. Don't bother hauling out the patio furniture, it will taste just as good if you eat it inside.

### 831

Read *Merry Christmas, Big Hungry Bear!* By Don Wood.

### 832

Make peppermint bark ice cream sodas. Add 3 tablespoons chocolate syrup each into 4 tall glasses. Add ¼ cup milk and 1 cup seltzer to each glass, then stir until foamy. Add 2 scoops of mint chocolate chip ice cream to each glass. Top with peppermint bark pieces and, if desired, a dollop of whipped cream.

### 833

If you have younger kids, set up a Christmas tree decorating station with a small tree of their own. Be sure to include non-breakable ornaments and plenty of garlands so they can decorate their tree as many times as they want.

### 834
Make holiday refrigerator magnets. You can easily pick up magnets at your local craft store and use air-dry clay to make festive shapes like Christmas trees, presents, and more.

### 835
Treat yourself to a festive dessert out at a restaurant one night.

### 836
Why not ask your elderly neighbor if they would like to join your family in cutting down a tree this year? Lending a hand in cutting down the tree and setting it up for someone who might not be able to is a great way to spread good cheer.

### 837
Make choco-mint shakes. Put 4 mint Oreo cookies in a strong plastic bag and crush them. In a blender, combine 2 cups vanilla ice cream, ½ cup milk, 1 tablespoon semi-sweet chocolate chips, and crushed cookies. Blend on high until combined. Divide into tall glasses and top with the crushed candy cane or peppermints.

### 838
Make a gin Christmas cocktail. Combine 2 oz. gin, 1 oz. cranberry simple syrup, and juice of ½ lemon in a mason jar and stir. Add 6 oz. hot mint tea, stir, and garnish with a peppermint stick and slice of lemon.

# 839
# Make your own Christmas crackers.

## Tools
Toilet paper rolls
Confetti or small gifts to put inside
Tissue paper
Ribbon or string
Scissors
Tape

## Directions
· Fill each toilet paper roll with small gifts or confetti and roll in tissue paper. Tie off each end with a ribbon and curl with scissors. Tape the edge of the tissue paper closed.

· To use, have two people pull on opposite ends of the cracker. The person who gets the side with the roll when it busts open gets to keep the gifts inside, or they can be shared.

**Tip:** While traditional Christmas crackers include cheesy jokes and trivia facts, you can switch things up by including fortunes or short poems.

# 840
# Make holiday popcorn balls.

## Ingredients

7 quarts popped popcorn
1 cup granulated sugar
1 cup light corn syrup
¼ cup water
¼ teaspoon salt
3 tablespoons unsalted butter
1 teaspoon vanilla extract
Festive sprinkles of choice

## Directions

- Heat the oven to 200°F. Place the popcorn on a large baking sheet and place in the oven to keep warm.

- In a heavy-bottomed saucepan, add the sugar, corn syrup, water, and salt. Cook over medium heat until the mixture is 235°F.

- Remove from heat, add the butter and vanilla, and stir until the butter is melted. Remove the popcorn from the oven and pour the mixture over the popcorn, stirring until evenly coated. Add the sprinkles.

- Once cool enough to handle, shape the popcorn into palm-sized balls, using cold water to keep your hands from sticking to the candy. Allow to cool until hardened.

### 841

Make homemade whipped cream to serve with your desserts. In the bowl of a stand mixer, combine heavy cream and granulated sugar, using ¼ cup of sugar for every 16 oz. of cream. Using the whisk attachment, start mixing on low speed and gradually increase as the cream begins to whip, eventually reaching high speed. Mix until the cream reaches desired consistency and serve right away.

### 842

Have a Christmas Eve pizza party. You'll probably be cooking a big dinner the next day, so why not keep things simple and fun on Christmas Eve by ordering your favorite pizza?

### 843

Give your children their own set of "thank you" cards for Christmas and remind them to send thank you notes to all the family members who got them gifts this year.

### 844

Donate your Christmas tree to a farm or a zoo when you are done with it. Just make sure to remove all decorations from the tree before donating it.

### 845

Go big this year by wrapping your entire door in wrapping paper like a giant Christmas present.

### 846

Watch *Grandma Got Run Over by a Reindeer* (2000).

### 847

Build an ice castle by filling different containers with water and then freezing them. Then, stack the objects together to make an ice castle. If you're having trouble getting your building blocks to stick together, try adding a bit of salt to help melt the ice.

### 848

Play exquisite corpse. Each person writes down the first sentence of a Christmas story and then passes it to the person to their right, folding the paper so the last sentence is covered. The next person then writes whatever sentence they want, covering it as well before it goes to the next person. At the end, read your stories out loud to see what you came up with.

### 849

Learn the rhythm to the "Cups" song and do it to your favorite Christmas carols. "Jingle Bells" is an easy one to start with.

### 850

Make pomander spiced cider. Combine 5 cups apple cider, 1 pinch nutmeg, and 1 teaspoon sugar in a large pot and stir to combine over medium heat. Bring mixture to a soft boil. Add 1 fresh orange pomander and 3 cinnamon sticks, reduce heat, and simmer for 15 to 20 minutes before serving. For an adult treat, spike a mug with a shot of whiskey or bourbon.

### 851

Watch *Four Christmases* (2008).

It is, indeed, regenerated feeling— kindling not merely in the hall, but of charity

the season of
the season for
the fire of hospitality
the genial flame
in the heart.

—Washington Irving

# 852

## Make marshmallows.

Ingredients
  1 cup water
  3 packets of gelatin
  1½ cups granulated sugar
  1 cup light corn syrup
  Seeds of 2 vanilla beans
  Confectioners' sugar, for dusting

## Directions

- Place ½ cup of the water in the bowl of a stand mixer. Sprinkle the gelatin into the water and let the gelatin dissolve.

- Place the remaining water, sugar, and corn syrup in a saucepan and cook, while swirling the pan occasionally, over medium heat until the mixture is 240°F. Remove the pan from heat and let stand for 1 minute.

- Fit the stand mixer with the whisk attachment and run it at low speed while slowly pouring the contents of the saucepan down the side of the mixing bowl.

- Gradually increase the speed of the mixer until the mixture is white, fluffy, and glossy. Add the vanilla seeds and whisk to incorporate.

- Sift the confectioners' sugar over a greased 9 x 13-inch baking dish until the dish is completely coated. Pour the mixture into the baking dish and use a greased rubber spatula to even out the surface. Let stand for 6 hours.

- When ready to serve, dust a work surface, a knife, and your hands with confectioners' sugar. Transfer the block of marshmallow to the work surface, cut into cubes, and serve.

## 853

Make homemade caramel sauce. In a small saucepan, combine 1 cup granulated sugar, ¼ cup water, 3 tablespoons unsalted butter, and ½ teaspoon salt and cook over medium-high heat until it is light brown. Be sure not to stir the mixture; instead, gently swirl the pan a few times as it cooks. Reduce heat to medium and cook for about 3 to 5 minutes, or until the mixture caramelizes. Stir the mixture once or twice to make sure it does not burn.

## 854

Decorate cookies together as a family. Be sure to have the dough ready ahead of time so that all you have to do is cut, bake, and decorate.

## 855

Spend the afternoon watching all the movies in your favorite film franchise as a family.

## 856

Have each family member share what their favorite Christmas memory from that season has been. Write down the memories in a special notebook with their names and ages, so you can look over them for years to come.

## 857

Hold an international holiday candy sampling night. You can find plenty of international candies for sale online. You might even find a new favorite treat.

### 858

Reach out to loved ones who are not nearby by sending them some much-needed care items during the holiday season. This is a great way to spread Christmas cheer.

### 859

Order a tray of creampuffs from an Italian bakery to have at Christmas. If you can't get them fresh, you can always find them frozen at your local grocery store.

### 860

If you have a coffee lover in your household, get them their own dedicated coffee mug complete with a sample of their favorite coffee to go with Christmas breakfast.

### 861

Make potpourri gift jars. Fill individual mason jars with one portion of Dried Fruit Potpourri (see page 271). Cut 6 x 6-inch squares of burlap or other holiday themed fabric and secure over the lid of the jar with ribbon or twine. Write or type directions for simmering potpourri on a small card and punch a hole in the corner. Attach a card to each jar, using ribbon or twine. For an extra festive gift, tie a sprig of evergreen to the outside of each jar.

### 862

Learn how to use simple looms to make your own hats, scarves, and more, then donate the results to your local charity.

# 863
## Make an ice candle holder.

Tools

    1 large container
    1 smaller container that fits inside the large container
    Tape
    Natural decorations of choice (like pine needles and holly)
    1 LED or wax tea light

## Directions

- Begin by placing the smaller container inside the larger one and filling water around the smaller container so that it floats. When the rims of the two containers are level, secure the smaller container in the center with tape.

- Fill in the rest of the space between the two containers with water. If you wish to add decorations to the candle, you can drop leaves, dried flowers, rocks, or any other desired trinkets into the water and position them to your liking.

- Place the candle in the freezer overnight, or outside if temperatures are below freezing. Once the ice has frozen solid, remove the tape and pop the candle out of its mold. If it has trouble coming out, you can run the outside of the large container under warm water until the ice detaches.

- Place your candle on a railing or stump outside where you can see in through the window, add the tea light, and light.

### 864

Make tin foil snowflakes. Instead of cutting your snowflakes out of the foil, shred tinfoil into tiny pieces and glue them onto a piece of construction paper in the shape of a snowflake. You can add multiple snowflakes per sheet of paper for a shimmering snowy scene.

### 865

Play two truths and a lie (Christmas edition). Have each player list two Christmas gifts they've actually received, and one that is a lie. Have each player try and guess which gift is the lie. The guessers get one point for every lie they find, and the liar gets one point for each person they fool with their lie.

### 866

Record a Christmas-themed voicemail for your family phone.

### 867

Keep track of all your recipes in a notebook where you record when you made each recipe, how it turned out, and if you plan to make it again. This will eliminate any frustrating guesswork as to which pie crust recipe worked great last year, or which gravy recipe was a total disaster.

### 868

Write encouraging letters to each other in the months before Christmas and then mail them so they arrive around the holidays for a wholesome surprise.

## 869

Have an at-home makeover party. See who can do the most festive makeup, hairstyles, and nail polish and be sure to take pictures of the results for your Christmas scrapbook.

## 870

Make sugar plums.
Heat oven to 350°F. Wash and dry 6 ripe plums thoroughly. Combine 1 cup granulated sugar with nutmeg and/or cinnamon, to taste. Place 2 egg whites in a bowl and whisk in 1 tablespoon water. Use a pastry brush to cover each plum with the egg wash, then roll the plums in the flavored sugar. Transfer sugared plums to a well-greased baking dish and bake for 15 minutes. Serve with fresh cream.

## 871

Read *The Church Mice at Christmas* by Graham Oakley.

## 872

Host an eggnog tasting party. You can serve different types of eggnog or have everyone make their own favorite holiday beverages to share.

## 873

Have everyone make a prediction for what will happen between now and next Christmas. Make sure to write them down to see if they come true.

## 874

Have a Christmas carol sing-along together in the car.

# 875
# Bake a jumbo cookie and eat it like a pie.

## Ingredients
2 sticks of unsalted butter, at room temperature
½ cup granulated sugar
1 cup brown sugar
2 eggs
2 teaspoons vanilla extract
1 teaspoon baking soda
2 teaspoons hot water
½ teaspoon salt
2½ cups flour
2 cups semisweet chocolate chips

## Directions
- Preheat the oven to 375°F. Heat a 12-inch cast-iron skillet in the oven while making the batter.

- In a large bowl, beat the butter and sugars together until light and fluffy. Add the eggs one at a time, being sure to combine thoroughly before proceeding. Stir in the vanilla.

- Dissolve the baking soda in the hot water and add to the batter with the salt. Stir in the flour and chocolate chips.

- Remove the skillet from the oven and put the batter in it, smoothing the top with a spatula.
- Put the skillet in the oven and cook until golden brown, about 15 minutes.

### 876

Make a virgin mudslide cocktail. Wet the rim of a Hurricane glass or a mason jar and dip it into chocolate shavings. In a blender, combine 1 oz. heavy cream, 2 to 3 scoops of vanilla ice cream, a dash of Monin amaretto syrup, and chocolate syrup, to taste, and puree until smooth. Pour into the glass and garnish with whipped cream and a maraschino cherry.

### 877

Have a Christmas decoration hunt where everyone tries to find the weirdest Christmas decorations possible. Whoever finds the weirdest item gets to choose who has to display the decoration.

### 878

Gift a loved one new winter gear.

### 879

Make Christmas bunting by decorating red or green paper or fabric triangles and stringing them together around your home.

### 880

Use special holiday mugs for the Christmas season. Give each family member a special Christmas mug to help make the season feel even more festive.

### 881

Learn your favorite Christmas carol in American Sign Language.

## 882

Dreaming of a white Christmas? Make paper snowflakes to hang on the doors and windows in your house. Use a compass to make a circle on a large piece of white printer paper. Cut out the circle and fold it in half. Fold in half again. The more times you fold the paper the more detailed your snowflake will be. Begin cutting away at the snowflake, making sure that at least some of the folded edges stay intact. Unfold carefully and display.

## 883

Check to see if any restaurants near you are running Christmas specials this year and try out their seasonal dishes.

## 884

Color an adult coloring book to help relax during the holidays. You can even find a winter- or holiday-themed one.

## 885

Make classic soda bread. Preheat oven to 430°F. In a bowl, combine 4½ cups all-purpose flour, 1¾ cups buttermilk, 1 teaspoon baking soda, and 1 teaspoon salt. Transfer to a clean surface and knead for 3 to 5 minutes. Form into a ball and transfer to a baking dish lined with parchment paper. Flatten the dough into a thick disk, then slash a deep cross on top of the loaf. Bake for 20 minutes, then reduce heat to 340°F and bake for another 20 to 25 minutes.

Christmas is
stuffed with

# a stocking
# sugary goodness.

—Mo Rocca

# 886
# Make mug cakes and decorate them.

## Ingredients
¼ cup all-purpose flour
¼ cup granulated sugar
2 tablespoons unsweetened cocoa powder
⅛ teaspoon baking soda
⅛ teaspoon salt
3 tablespoons milk
2 tablespoons canola oil
1 tablespoon water
¼ teaspoon vanilla extract
Chocolate chips (optional), to taste

## Directions
· Mix the flour, sugar, cocoa powder, baking soda, and salt in a large, microwave-safe mug. Add the milk, canola oil, water, and vanilla extract and stir well. If desired, add the chocolate chips and stir.

· Cook in the microwave for about 1 minute 45 seconds, or until the cake is done in the middle. The cook time can vary depending on the type of microwave.

# 887
## Make no-bake cookies.

### Ingredients

1½ cups granulated sugar
¼ cup honey
½ teaspoon salt
½ cup whole milk
1 stick unsalted butter
¼ cup unsweetened cocoa powder
3 cups old-fashioned rolled oats
1 cup creamy peanut butter
1 teaspoon vanilla extract

### Directions

- Combine the sugar, honey, salt, milk, butter, and cocoa powder in a saucepan and cook over medium heat. Once everything is combined, cook for an additional 1 to 2 minutes.

- Remove the saucepan from heat and stir in the oats, peanut butter, and vanilla extract. Let cool for two minutes.

- Line a baking sheet with parchment paper. Use a tablespoon to scoop the cookies onto the baking sheet. Place in the refrigerator and chill for an hour before serving.

### 888

Use whatever vegetables you have in the fridge to leave a healthy snack outside for Santa's reindeer. They'll be sure to remember your house next year.

### 889

Make baked potatoes in a campfire. Begin by cutting a slit in all potatoes being cooked and slathering the outside with butter. Wrap the buttered potatoes in tin foil and place them in the hot coals of the fire. Cook for 30 minutes, rotating the potatoes several times. After 30 minutes, remove the potatoes and use a fork to carefully unwrap and test. If the potato is not fully cooked, return it to the fire for 10 more minutes and repeat until fully cooked.

### 890

Have a gift-stacking relay. Each team is given 10 presents, divided between two tables across the room from each other. The first relay runner goes to the opposite table and sets their gift down before returning to the first table. The second relay runner goes to the opposite table and stacks their gift on the first gift, handing this to their third team member. Whichever team stacks and carries all 10 gifts without dropping any, wins.

### 891

Create your own popcorn carols by having one person sing a line, and the next person sing the next line. The more ridiculous the better.

### 892

Plan a special Christmas-themed date night with your significant other. You could book a table at your favorite restaurant, go ice skating, look at Christmas lights, or head to the movies.

### 893

Have an ornament relay race. Set up a relay course of your choosing. Split into two teams. Give each team a plastic ornament and enough spoons for each player. The goal of the relay is to have each player run the relay without dropping the ornament, then pass it to their teammate using only their spoon. If the ornament is dropped, the racer must start the course over. The team that finishes first wins.

### 894

Participate in a charity swim. Many places across the country host swimming challenges where participants are asked to swim in a chilly body of water to raise money for charity. This can be a good-spirited and often humorous way to raise money for a good cause, but remember it's only fun if you're not in any danger.

### 895

Bake mini gingerbread houses for your hot chocolate mugs.

### 896

Write and produce a Christmas play to perform in front of other family members.

# 897

## Make Santa strawberries.

### Ingredients
1 pint strawberries
2 cups whipped cream
Chocolate sprinkles

### Directions
- Remove the leafy end of each strawberry, making sure they can stand up evenly. Then, cut off the tip of the strawberry to make Santa's hat.

- Place a spoonful of whipped cream on top of each strawberry, then add the hat on top. Add a small dot of whipped cream to the top of the hat to make a pom-pom.

- Using a toothpick, carefully add two sprinkles to the center dollop of whipped cream to make eyes. Then, add two tiny dots of whipped cream to the body of the strawberry for buttons. Enjoy immediately or refrigerate.

# 898
## Make fondue.

### Ingredients
1 lb. Gruyère cheese, grated
½ lb. Emmentaler cheese, grated
½ lb. Gouda cheese, grated
2 teaspoons cornstarch
1 garlic clove
1 cup chicken broth
1 tablespoon lemon juice
Salt, pepper, and grated nutmeg, to taste
Bread or crackers of choice

### Directions
- In a bowl, toss the cheeses with the cornstarch until the cheese is well-coated.

- Cut the garlic clove in half. Rub the inside of a crockpot or fondue pot with the garlic, then add the chicken broth and lemon juice and bring to a simmer over low heat.

- Add the cheese mixture all at once. Using a wooden spoon, stir over medium-low heat until the cheese is melted and smooth, about 5 to 10 minutes.

- Season with salt, pepper, and grated nutmeg. Dip your favorite snacks into the fondue and enjoy.

### 899
Read *Little Women*
by Louisa May Alcott.

### 900
Sleep late on Christmas
morning. This works best if
you don't have any young
children in the house.

### 901
"Adopt" a wild animal for
the holidays through your
favorite wildlife foundation.

### 902
Make miniature
candy snowmen using mini
marshmallows for the body,
mini pretzel sticks for the
arms, mini M&Ms for the
eyes, and a chocolate
chip for the hat.

### 903
For each Christmas card
that you send, make sure to
include a personalized note
that reminds the recipient why
they are special to you, or why
you appreciate having
them in your life.

### 904
Take a carriage ride
through the snow.

### 905
Listen to Christmas music
from around the world.

### 906
For a Christmas morning
surprise, top your pancakes
with whipped cream and
crushed peppermint pieces.

**907**
Give the gift of music by gifting someone lessons for their instrument of choice.

**908**
Make reindeer feed. In a large bowl, combine 4 cups oats with red and green sugar sprinkles. Fill individual bags or jars with ½ cup portions of the mixture. On Christmas Eve, help children spread the feed outside for Santa's reindeer.

**909**
Give a "_____ in a jar" gift by making a miniature kit inside a jar to suit the interests of the person you are gifting it to. You can make sewing kits, fishing kits, cooking kits, and more.

**910**
Read *The Little Drummer Boy* by Ezra Jack Keats.

**911**
Try to pay it forward this Christmas by practicing kindness to strangers and loved ones. This might mean paying for the car behind you in the drive-through or making sure to tell someone you're proud of them when you see them doing a good job.

**912**
Listen to *Elvis' Christmas Album*.

**913**
Read the poem "In the bleak midwinter" by Christina Rossetti.

# 914
# Make homemade holiday treats for your dog.

**Ingredients**
1½ cups oat flour, plus more for dusting
1½ cups brown rice flour
1 teaspoon baking powder
1 egg
½ cup chicken broth
Smooth peanut butter, for filling

## Directions

- Preheat the oven to 350°F. Combine all the ingredients except for the broth and peanut butter. Slowly add the broth, mixing until the dough forms. If it is too dry, add more broth, if it is too wet, add more flour.

- Roll the dough out onto a lightly floured surface until it is ¼ inch thick. Use a round cookie cutter to cut circles in the dough. Place a small amount of the peanut butter between each round, then gather the edges together to create a small bundle.

- Line a baking sheet with parchment paper and add the treats, keeping them about ¼ inch apart.

- Bake for 25 to 30 minutes or until golden brown. Transfer to a wire rack and allow to cool completely. Store in an airtight container in the refrigerator or give to your furry friend immediately.

I heard the bells
Their old, familiar
wild and sweet
Of peace on earth,

on Christmas Day
carols play. And
The words repeat
good-will to men!

—Henry Wadsworth Longfellow

### 915

Go Christmas caroling inside a dorm building with a group of college students.

### 916

Spot some mistletoe. Did you know that mistletoe must grow off of a host plant in order to survive? That means you can often find it growing in clumps that look like large spheres on other trees.

### 917

Make sure there's a bit of Christmas cheer in every part of the house by using special Christmas-themed shower curtains and towels throughout the holidays. You can even set out Christmas-scented soap.

### 918

Replace the lampshades in your house with Christmas-themed ones to take your decorating skills to the next level.

### 919

Include your extended family in your family Christmas card photos this year.

### 920

Listen to the soundtrack to *A Charlie Brown Christmas*.

### 921

Instead of wrapping paper, use upcycled brown paper bags or newspaper to wrap gifts. You can decorate the paper with paints, glitter, or stamps.

## 922

Make a Christmas photo booth complete with cut out masks, props, and backgrounds. You can set a camera or your phone on a timer or even use your computer as a photography station.

## 923

Roast some chestnuts. Preheat oven to 425°F. Use a knife to cut an "X" in the shell of each nut. Make sure that you slice all the way through the shell to the flesh of the chestnut. Once all the chestnuts have been scored, place them scored-side up on a large baking sheet and cook for 25 to 30 minutes. Remove from the oven. Once the chestnuts are cool enough to handle, peel and enjoy.

## 924

You've heard of Christmas in July, but what about July at Christmas? Give your holiday party a sunny, tropical theme this Christmas, complete with bathing suits and beach decorations.

## 925

Get reindeer antlers and a red nose for your car.

## 926

Make an Evergreen Pine cocktail. Pour 1 (12 oz.) can of Dr. Pepper into a pint glass, drop a shot glass containing 1 oz. London Dry Gin into the glass, and drink immediately.

## 927

Volunteer at your local soup kitchen.

# 928
# Make peppermint-coated chocolate-dipped pretzels.

### Ingredients
　　1 (12 oz.) bag of semisweet chocolate chips
　　1 teaspoon vegetable shortening (no substitutions)
　　20 pretzel rods
　　Peppermint candies, crushed to shards

## Directions

- In a strong plastic bag, use a hammer or rolling pin to crush the peppermint candies into shards. Put on a flat plate and set aside. Line a baking sheet with parchment paper. Set aside.

- In a double boiler or in a bowl over simmering water, melt the chocolate chips until just melted. Alternately, put the chips in a microwave-safe bowl and melt in 20- to 30-second increments until just melted.

- Dip the pretzel rods into the melted chocolate about halfway, tilting the bowl to easily dip. Use the side of the bowl to remove excess. Let cool for a minute while excess drips into the bowl, then roll the stick in the candy pieces. Place the finished pretzel rods on the baking sheet.

- Refrigerate for 20 minutes or until set. Store in airtight container at room temperature.

### 929
Go curling.

### 930
Fill water balloons with small toys and then put them in the freezer. Once the water is frozen, have your kids race to see who can break their prizes out the fastest using a hair dryer or water (not both).

### 931
Have a Christmas card party. Form an assembly line with the whole family and pass the cards around the table for everyone to sign. Assign each family member a job such as writing out addresses, stamping and licking envelopes, putting school photos inside, and so on.

### 932
Read Christmas stories and let your kids color Christmas pictures while they listen.

### 933
Make holiday ice cubes. Drop bits of dried cranberries, mint leaves and fresh rosemary into each hole in an ice cube tray. Cover with water, freeze, and enjoy.

### 934
If your kids don't have any snow to play in, make cloud dough snow instead. Divide 8 cups all-purpose flour into 4 bowls. Add ¼ cup vegetable oil to each bowl of flour and mix by hand until combined. Keep in a flat storage bin between uses.

### 935

Make an eggnog spiced chai. Slowly whisk ½ cup warmed eggnog into a mug containing ½ cup brewed chai tea. Whisk in ½ teaspoon cinnamon and enjoy.

### 936

If you live in a place that is not covered in snow during December, organize a street cleanup in your town.

### 937

Have a secret Santa note exchange where each person is assigned a family member that they will write a positive note. Then, place these notes in each other's stockings on Christmas morning.

### 938

Make Christmas trees using pipe cleaners.

### 939

Fill a mason jar with Christmas candy and have everyone guess how many candies are in the jar. The winner gets a prize or gets to keep the jar of candy.

### 940

Get a bunch of succulents and decorate them with little Santa hats or mini Christmas lights.

### 941

Shovel your neighbor's driveway the next time it snows.

# 942
# Make hot chocolate stirring spoons.

## Ingredients
   3 cups chocolate pieces of choice
   Plastic or metal spoons
   1 cup crushed peppermints (optional)
   Sprinkles or other edible decorations (optional)

### Directions

- Cover a cookie sheet with a piece of parchment paper. Stir the chocolate in a double boiler until all pieces have melted and the chocolate is smooth.

- Turn off the heat. Take a spoon and dip into the chocolate, leaving the handle exposed. Remove from chocolate and let the layer harden for a moment before dipping the spoon again. Repeat this process until the chocolate reaches desired thickness around the spoon.

- On the last dip, quickly move the spoon over an empty bowl and sprinkle with desired toppings before the chocolate hardens.

- Transfer the finished spoon to the cookie sheet to cool. Repeat with remaining spoons and chocolate. If the chocolate starts to harden in the pan, return to heat until the chocolate is smooth again.

### 943

Find out if Santa is making an appearance at your local mall or Christmas tree farm and plan a visit.

### 944

Let your kids cook a family dinner over the holidays (with supervision for younger kids, of course).

### 945

Watch the Christmas classic, *It's a Wonderful Life* (1946). Make sure to have a box of tissues on hand.

### 946

Decorate your glasses for the holidays using pipe cleaners, jingle bells, or anything else you can think of.

### 947

Look for animal prints out in nature. If you live somewhere where it snows, you'd be surprised just how many animals are around during the winter.

### 948

Make virgin apple pie cocktails. Combine ¾ cup apple cider and ¼ cup cream soda in a glass, and then add a dash of cinnamon. Stir until well combined and garnish with dollop of ice cream, 1 cinnamon stick, and 1 star anise pod.

### 949

Go on a bus tour of a city to see all the Christmas decorations.

### 950
Deliver gifts or cookies to first responders near you.

### 951
If you know anyone who may be alone for the holidays, invite them to join in your holiday celebrations.

### 952
If you have a pet fish, decorate the tank for the holidays. Most pet stores have Christmas-themed, fish-friendly decorations to choose from.

### 953
If you're near New York City, visit the Empire State Building when it is lit up red and green for Christmas.

### 954
Watch *Home Alone* (1990).

### 955
Make ice cream cone Christmas trees. Mix green food coloring into 1 can vanilla frosting to create a nice green color. Turn ice cream cones upside down and line them up on a piece of parchment paper. Use a butter knife to cover each cone with frosting and decorate with sprinkles or your candy of choice. Strings of licorice and mini gum drops or M&Ms make great edible Christmas lights.

### 956
Watch *Rudolph the Red-Nosed Reindeer* (1964).

# 957
## Make white chocolate cocoa-mint truffles.

### Ingredients
  1 cup peppermint candy pieces
  ⅓ cup plus 2 tablespoons heavy cream
  1 tablespoon unsalted butter, at room temperature
  8 oz. white chocolate baking bars
  1 cup unsweetened shredded coconut

## Directions

- In a strong plastic bag, use a hammer or rolling pin to crush several peppermint candy pieces into fine shards. Pour the shards onto a plate and set aside.

- In a small saucepan, bring the cream to a simmer over medium heat, being careful not to let it boil. Add the butter and stir until melted. Add the white chocolate pieces, stirring constantly until completely melted and smooth.

- Remove from the heat and pour the chocolate-and-cream mixture into a shallow bowl. Allow to cool to room temperature, then cover with plastic wrap and refrigerate until firm, at least 2 hours.

- Line a baking sheet with wax or parchment paper. Use a small spoon to scoop out the chocolate and use your hands to roll the scoops into balls.

- Put the shredded coconut on a plate. Roll the balls in the candy shards and then in the coconut. Serve immediately or put in an airtight container and refrigerate.

Christmas is one's home carries in

a piece of
that one
one's heart.

—Freya Stark

### 958

Make reindeer head ornaments using corks, googly eyes, red pom-poms for the nose, and pipe cleaners for the antlers. Don't forget to add a loop of string to hang it up.

### 959

Take turns explaining Christmas movie plots badly while everyone else has to guess what movie you're referencing.

### 960

Make a magical snow scene using soap flakes mixed with water and Christmas decorations to create a scene of your choosing.

### 961

Read *Hercule Poirot's Christmas* by Agatha Christie.

### 962

Visit a winter carnival near you.

### 963

Make infused olive oil for Christmas gifts. Gently bruise garlic, twists of lemon peel, rosemary, thyme, basil, dill, sage, or other aromatics (making sure they have been thoroughly washed and dried). Place the add-ins inside a jar or bottle and fill with olive oil. Seal the container and leave for 2 weeks. Once the oil has reached the desired flavor, strain out the add-ins and preserve the rest of the oil.

### 964
Watch made-for-TV Christmas movies on different channels and vote on who makes the corniest ones around.

### 965
Go window-shopping during the holidays and rate your favorite window displays.

### 966
Instead of one large tree, give each family member a mini tree to decorate however they want.

### 967
Hide scratch tickets inside everyone's Christmas stocking this year.

### 968
Wake up early on Christmas morning and watch the sunrise.

### 969
Make a Lemon Champagne Fizz cocktail. Combine ½ oz. gin, ⅓ oz. lemon juice, and a pinch of caster sugar in a cocktail shaker filled with crushed ice and shake vigorously. Strain into a shot glass, top with 1 oz. Champagne, and garnish with lemon wedge.

### 970
Visit the grocery store the day after Christmas and pick up some discounted Christmas candy.

# 971
## Make white chocolate almond squares.

**Ingredients**
- 1 cup almonds, blanched and chopped
- 1 cup unsalted butter
- 1 cup dark brown sugar, firmly packed
- Yolk of 1 large egg, at room temperature
- 1 teaspoon vanilla extract
- 2 cups all-purpose flour
- ¼ teaspoon salt
- ½ lb. quality white chocolate, chopped

## Directions

- Preheat the oven to 350°F. Line a 9 x 13-inch baking pan with parchment paper. Place almonds on a baking sheet and toast for 5 to 7 minutes, until lightly browned.

- Combine the butter and sugar in a mixing bowl and beat at low speed with an electric mixer to blend. Increase the speed to high and beat for 3 to 4 minutes, until light and fluffy. Add the egg yolk and vanilla and beat for 1 minute. Slowly add the flour and salt and beat until a stiff dough forms. Pat the dough evenly into the baking pan and prick it with a fork. Place the pan on the middle rack in the oven and cook for 20 minutes, or until light brown.

- Remove the pan from the oven and scatter the white chocolate evenly over the crust. Return the pan to the oven for 1 minute, remove, and spread the chocolate into an even layer. Sprinkle the almonds on top, allow to cool in the pan, and then cut into bars.

**972**
Read *Olive, the Other Reindeer* by J. Otto Seibold.

**973**
Attend a Christmas- or winter-themed paint night.

**974**
Take a winter hike up a mountain and bring a thermos of hot chocolate to drink at the top.

**975**
Have a Christmas treat blindfold taste test. Blindfold each player, then have everyone try the same Christmas snack. Whoever gets the most snacks right, wins!

**976**
Host a holiday tea party.

**977**
Put a twist on classic eggnog with a coffee eggnog cocktail. In a blender, combine 1 teaspoon simple syrup, 2 oz. Scotch whisky, 1 oz. Kahlua, 6 oz. milk, 1 oz. half-and-half, ½ teaspoon instant coffee, 1 egg, and 1 cup ice and puree until smooth. Pour into a chilled Hurricane glass or divide between shot glasses, and then garnish with cinnamon.

**978**
Watch *The Year Without a Santa Claus* (1974).

## 979

Make a white chocolate peppermint-tini. Put about ¼ cup of marshmallow sundae topping on a small plate or saucer. Put ½ cup crushed white peppermint bark pieces on a separate small plate or saucer. Dip the rims of 2 glasses in the marshmallow and then into the peppermint bark. Use a teaspoon to drizzle additional marshmallow topping on the inside of each glass. Combine 4 oz. vanilla vodka, 2 oz. peppermint schnapps, and 2 oz. white chocolate liquor in a cocktail shaker filled about halfway with crushed ice. Shake for a minute or so. Divide the liquid between glasses and serve.

## 980

Go for a dog sled ride.

## 981

Carve festive shapes into bars of soap using dental floss and toothpicks.

## 982

Get breakfast with Santa. Many locations offer a special breakfast with Santa this time of year. Check your local newspaper or online to see if there is one near you.

## 983

If you have kids in your family, take time each night to read a Christmas bedtime story leading up to Christmas.

# 984
# Make a Hot Toddy Margarita.

## Ingredients
2 oz. Añejo tequila
¾ oz. orange liqueur
½ oz. agave nectar
¼ oz. fresh lime juice
¼ oz. fresh orange juice
1 oz. hot water (170°F)
1 cinnamon stick, for garnish
1 to 2 whole cloves, for garnish

## Directions
· Combine the tequila, orange liqueur, agave nectar, lime juice, and orange juice in an insulated glass. Top with the hot water and garnish with the cinnamon stick and cloves.

# 985

## Make caprese skewers as a Christmas appetizer.

### Ingredients
Small mozzarella balls
Basil leaves
Cherry tomatoes
Skewers
Balsamic reduction
Salt and pepper, to taste

### Directions
· Place each of the three ingredients on a skewer and arrange skewers decoratively on a platter. Drizzle with balsamic and finish with salt and pepper.

### 986
Try some peppermint-flavored seltzer water.

### 987
Take your friend's children out Christmas shopping for the day so they have the opportunity to get a gift for their mom or dad that will be a complete surprise.

### 988
Make a Snow Bowl cocktail. In a cocktail shaker filled with ice, combine 1 part gin, 1 part white chocolate liqueur, and a splash of crème de menthe, shake well, and strain into a rocks glass filled with ice. Garnish with a dusting of nutmeg.

### 989
Add glitter to white playdough to make snow playdough. Then, make playdough snowmen to decorate your home.

### 990
Get together a small group of close friends and make dinner together.

### 991
Give a good quality water bottle or travel mug to a loved one.

### 992
Get Christmas-themed lawn gnomes and use them to decorate your yard.

### 993
Watch *Elf* (2003).

### 994
Keep a bowl of shelled nuts on the counter to snack on throughout the holidays. Don't forget to keep a nutcracker nearby.

### 995
Treat yourself to a specialty coffee brand.

### 996
Gift a friend an I.O.U. for the next time they need a helping hand. That extra bit of help can be so much more valuable than giving them more stuff.

### 997
Get your pet a Christmas sweater and include them in your family Christmas photo.

### 998
Have a Christmas dance party.

### 999
Take turns reading your kids' favorite Christmas stories using funny voices.

### 1000
Surprise a family member by doing a home improvement project as their Christmas gift.

# 1001

## Make sweet potato pie.

### Ingredients
  2 cups sweet potatoes, mashed
  1 (12 oz.) can of evaporated milk
  2 eggs, lightly beaten
  ½ cup granulated sugar
  ½ teaspoon salt
  1 teaspoon cinnamon
  ¼ teaspoon ground ginger
  ¼ teaspoon ground nutmeg
  1 stick of unsalted butter
  1 cup light brown sugar
  1 ball pie crust dough

## Directions

- Preheat the oven to 400°F. In a large bowl, add the sweet potatoes, evaporated milk, eggs, sugar, salt, cinnamon, ginger, and nutmeg and stir until combined.

- Place a cast-iron skillet over medium heat and melt the butter in it. Add the brown sugar and cook, while stirring constantly, until the sugar is dissolved. Remove pan from heat.

- Pour the butter-and-brown sugar into a 9-inch pie plate. Roll out the crust and gently place it over the butter-and-brown sugar mixture. Fill with the sweet potato mixture, place the pie in the oven, and bake for 15 minutes. Reduce the heat to 325°F and bake for an additional 30 to 45 minutes until the filling is firm and a toothpick inserted in the middle comes out clean. Remove the pie from the oven and allow to cool before serving.

Oh, no, Christmas unless you Christmas is a